D1598231

Josef W. Seifert

Visualization – Presentation – Moderation

A Practical Guide to successful presentation
and the Facilitation of Business Processes

Josef W. Seifert

Visualization
Presentation
Moderation

A Practical Guide to successful presentation
and the Facilitation of Business Processes

2nd Edition

Josef W. Seifert
Langenbrucker Straße 4
85309 Pörnbach/Puch
Germany

Printed in the Federal Republic
of Germany.
Printed on acid-free paper.

This book was carefully produced.
Nevertheless, author and publisher do not warrant the information contained therein to be free of errors. Readers are advised to keep in mind that statements, data, illustrations, procedural details or other items may inadvertently be inaccurate.

Library of Congress Card No.: applied for
A catalogue record for this book is available from the British Library.
Die Deutsche Bibliothek – CIP Cataloguing-in-Publication-Data
A catalogue record for this publication is available from Die Deutsche Bibliothek

© WILEY-VCH Verlag GmbH,
D-69469 Weinheim
(Federal Republic of Germany).
2002

Cover Design
ADVERMA, Rohrbach

Cover illustration and chapter cover sheets
Design House, Laufer & Zahs, Nußloch

Text illustrations
Peter Kaste, Erlangen

Setup and layout
Josef W. Seifert, Puch/
ADVERMA, Rohrbach

Printed by
rgg Print Medien GmbH,
Braunschweig

ISBN 3-527-50034-0

Contents

Foreword to the First German Edition

Most people have, in a manner of speaking, been "damaged" by school: over the years they have experienced that "learning" and "teaching" are primarily associated with "speaking" and "speech." Oral contributions by teachers and pupils are still the focal point of didactic activity wherever the educational process is institutionally guided. This "learning environment" has one-sidedly channeled our natural learning habits towards the spoken word and passively receptive learning, while uniformly influencing our expectations in learning situations in the same way.

Now if in turn the pupils become teachers, company instructors, or management-level employees, they often merely "exchange roles": whereas they previously spent years drilling themselves to listen to the teacher speaking, they now for their part quickly grow "accustomed" to presenting issues, instructions, and solutions to problems and to practicing the "art of lecturing."

Among the many possible detrimental effects of this, two are particularly tragic: one is the conception that what was said was also understood, and the other is the notion that the task of the pupil or co-worker must be confined to listening and/or to following instructions.

The present book is an excellent guide to helping to dispel this "speechification." The author has compiled a wealth of proven methods and techniques of visualization, presentation, and moderation that are useful in conveying understandable information and that offer practically oriented aids for working together to solve problems in seminars and workgroups. In doing this he uses clear concepts and structures.

That is why this book has a great deal to do with the true "art" of didactic activity.

Theo Hülshoff, Professor of the University of Landau, Germany

Preface to the 2nd English Edition

Visualization, presentation, and moderation are tasks faced by employees of modern organizations more and more frequently. The importance of this topic is evidenced by the growing interest in corresponding practice sessions and complete training courses.

During my work in moderation and training techniques I have been asked repeatedly about literature presenting the topics of visualization and presentation and/or moderation in a concise, realistic form. This is why, in 1989, I wrote the present book, which in the meantime has been translated into several languages and rolled off the presses over 100,000 times. I completely revised the book for the fourth impression and made a number of changes and supplements for the sixth impression.

For the 16th German impression I have revised the book again and added to it, so that it is once again "up-to-date" with regard to both content and design. This book is the unabridged and completely revised second English Edition. For example, the graphics have been redone using modern graphics programs, the topic "electronic media" has been added, and the presentation has been made more attractive.

In this edition too, as from the beginning, the three closely related subject areas visualization, presentation, and moderation are again presented together in one volume rather than distinctly isolated from one another, in order to provide the user with a collection of the most important basic principles, rules, and helpful hints, which together make up a comprehensive "dry run."

The focal point of the treatments is the "how to," that is, the concrete stimulus for practical application. In this way I wish to encourage you, the reader, to use the book as a reference work and a workbook, to make your own notes in it and thus to let it become a practical tool for your everyday work.

Have fun reading and browsing through this book. I also hope you find it useful.

Puch, Germany, Februar 2002

Josef W. Seifert

1 Visualization

1.1 Why Visualization?

A picture is worth a thousand words, as the saying goes. Even though recent studies have shown that every individual has a preferred input channel and that it is not always the visual one, the indisputable fact remains that people are "seeing animals." Most people are (at least partly) "visual types." Apart from that, a visual representation does in fact say more than anyone could express in a thousand words; just think of the visual aspects of day-to-day interaction with one another, the area of non-verbal communication.

Here is another interesting fact, the "assimilation rate:"

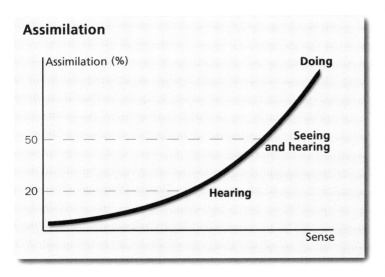

Fig. 1. Assimilation rate

As this illustration shows, we assimilate 30% more from a presentation when pictorial representations (images, symbols, the written word) are used. The total advantages of visualization can only be guessed at.

But what exactly is "visualization"? Visualization means the "pictorial representation" of something, which can include factual statements, emotions, and processes. This optical documentation does not have to replace the spoken word. Its aim is rather:

- to focus the receivers' attention
- to involve the observers
- to reduce the amount of speaking required
- to give the audience orientation aids
- to make information easy (or easier) to grasp
- to emphasize crucial points
- to expand on and supplement what has been said
- to promote assimilation
- to encourage comments

There are no limits to personal creativity in visualization; however, you should know the fundamentals of pictorial representation and take them into account. This includes knowing about ...

... planning a visualization
... building blocks of a visualization
... rules for composing a visualization

1.2 Planning a Visualization

As a rule a thorough concept must be developed before a visualization can become a reality. Depending on the situation, it may or may not be possible to do this to a satisfactory degree. Even if very little preparation is possible, however, you should not entirely do without visualization and its positive effects. If you have enough time and/or the representation is particularly important, you should definitely allow yourself plenty of time for preparation.

Very intensive preparation is a prerequisite for good, "impromptu" representations during a presentation, since the presenter must have a previously developed image in his or her "mind's eye" (and/or a light sketch in pencil on the page).

As in the case of the good old essay of our school days, the first step to take in thorough preparation of a representation is to gather material. First of all, collect any information on the topic that could be useful in any way. Then, in a second step, select the items from this wealth of material that seem to be most important (rough selection).

The third step is to further condense the items found in the rough selection. For this you could use the following key questions:

- What do I want to represent? (content)

- What is the purpose of the representation? (goal)

- Whom do I want to inform or convince? (target group)

Only after this planning stage do we deal with the visualization itself, and the question to be answered now is how the planned contents are to be represented and by what means.

1.3 Building Blocks of a Visualization

To produce a visualization, you need, on the one hand, elements of content, with which the information can be logically constructed, and, on the other, media on which the visualization physically takes shape. Together these can be called the "building blocks" of a visualization. They are used to compose an overall representation in accordance with certain rules.

The media most commonly used in (company) practice are:

- pin board (and packing paper)
- flip chart (stand and paper)
- overhead projector (and transparencies (acetates))
- beamer etc. (and PC/laptop)

Examples of design elements are:

- text
- free-style graphics and symbols
- diagrams

The design elements are equally well suited for use with any media – the design rules are the same.

The media differ from one another in terms of usefulness, depending on the occasion and purpose of their employment. Therefore, in the following pages you will find first of all a brief description of each medium. Directly following that I will discuss the design elements mentioned above. The rules of design are described in Section 1.4, "Composing a Visualization."

1.3.1 Media for Visualization (Information Carriers)

Pin Board

A pin board is a board of expanded polystyrene, approximately 150 – 125 cm (5 – 4 ft), to which special sheets of paper can be pinned. The board is set in a frame and is either mounted on the wall or has a stand and can be moved throughout the room as required. Collapsible or foldable versions with an accompanying carrying bag are also available. The pin board can then be transported in any medium-sized car.

Pin board paper is either brown or white and is written on using special fiber-tipped pens with calligraphic tips.

Pin boards are especially well suited for work in small groups of up to 20 participants.

Cards (rectangles, circles, and ovals) used in moderation sessions can be used as additional material here. They are cut out of thin cardboard and available in a variety of sizes and colors.

The pin board lends itself well both to the presentation of previously prepared representations and to keeping track of the development of content. Pin boards are the main visualization media for moderation sessions.

Fig. 2. Pin board

Flip Chart

A flip chart stand is a portable device for holding special flipchart paper (approx. 70 – 100 cm; 28 – 39 in.). It is particularly useful for work in very small to small groups of up to about 10 people.

Special fiber-tip pens (just as for pin-board paper) are used to write on the paper.

Representations on a flip chart can be prepared in advance or developed as the situation demands. They can remain in full view during the entire work session and be used again later.

The possibility of keeping a representation visible during the whole session is a big plus point of flip charts.

In both presentations and moderation sessions flip charts are employed as useful "visualization workhorses."

Fig. 3. Flip chart

Overhead Projektor

The overhead projector (OHP) is widely used for projecting representations made on transparent films (acetates). The transparencies are letter size or A4 while the dimensions of the projected image depend on the size of the screen and the projector's distance from it. The OHP is suitable for presentations to both small and large groups. A particular feature is that a very large number of participants can be "served" at the same time – up to several hundred people, depending on the projector model.

In most cases the transparencies are produced with special software (for example, Microsoft's "PowerPoint") on a computer and printed out using a color printer. Transparencies or slides can also be directly projected from a PC by means of an LCD (liquid crystal display) panel. Then, the LCD panel is simply placed on the projector, instead of a transparency. A "provisional" solution is to use a so-called "feeder", which works in exactly the same way as the feeder of a photocopier, except in this case transparencies are transported, step by step. This can, of course, be controlled remotely.

Naturally, it is also possible to produce transparencies "manually", using special film markers (with washable or permanent ink). Especially suitable are markers with calligraphic tips (see "Tips for Working with Markers," page 22).

The transparencies can be prepared ahead of time or developed as the situation demands. Their long life and ease of transport are big plus points, particularly if representations are to be used repeatedly.

The disadvantage of the overhead projector as compared to the pin board and the flip chart: individual representations can be viewed only while actually being projected.

Fig. 4. Overhead projector

Beamer etc.

The beamer is a digital projector that can project overhead transparencies onto a screen directly from the (portable) computer that was used to produce the representation (using special software such as "PowerPoint" or "HarvardGraphics"). This makes printing out transparencies and placing them on an overhead projector superfluous.

With the digital projector, pictures for a presentation can now be "movies." Visualizations can now include dynamic elements: text and graphics can be completely or partially faded in or out, or "pixeled out," and speech, music, or even film sequences can be worked in … The transition to film is fluid. The process can be controlled remotely or by mouse. Photographs taken with a digital camera can be integrated into the visualization or (depending on the available hardware) directly projected.

Ultrasmall, powerful, light mini-laptops are ideal partners for data video projectors. Many models offer "plug and play"; they simply have to be plugged in to the computer – configuration and synchronization take place automatically.

The great advantage of this "perfect" technology is also its decisive disadvantage: its perfection. As the extent to which the technical possibilities are used increases, the presentation becomes more professional but also more sterile and "smooth." In the extreme case it becomes a "film show." The only thing missing then is popcorn …

As difficult as it is to "overdo" a "low-tech" presentation using pin board or flip chart, so easy it is to fall into this trap when using electric or electronic media, from overhead to digital projector.

By the way: For a brilliant representation the available projection surface is decisive. Therefore, if you are not quite sure that the equipment provided where the presentation is to be held is up to standard, it is better to take your own portable screen with you!

Fig. 5. Beamer etc.

... And What Else There Is:

The reasons for and aims of presentations are extremely complex. Which media could possibly be used or which are necessary has to be clarified for each individual situation. The ideal case is certainly that in which the presentation can be carried out "live" and "representation technology" need not be used at all. Placing a product on the table so that the original can be observed or even felt is certainly the optimum.

As this is often not possible, presenters have to rely on presentation technology and media. These include – as already presented – above all the pin board, flip chart, overhead projector, and PC with digital projector.

In addition there are some less common or widely used devices. These include the table flip chart, the LCD display for the PC, the "instant presenter" (a projector that can project a page of a book, for example), the (microprocessor-controlled) slide projector, the CCD mini color camera for live presentations of objects, for example, and combined devices, such as the "Copyboard" and "Copyflip", which, if wished, immediately print out in A4 format what has been written. The "ibid" allows data to be projected onto a flip chart with a sensitive surface using PC and beamer. Alterations made on the chart can then be immediately transferred to the computer. Up-to-date information about media for particular applications can be obtained from specialist shops and in the internet; innovations appear almost daily.

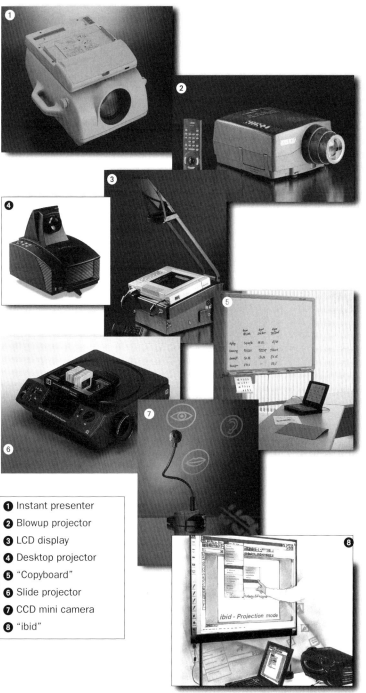

1 Instant presenter
2 Blowup projector
3 LCD display
4 Desktop projector
5 "Copyboard"
6 Slide projector
7 CCD mini camera
8 "ibid"

Fig. 6. Other media

Tips for Working with Felt-tip Pens

Before moving on to the design elements, at this point we would like to make just a few, but important, suggestions for working with felt-tip pens, which, despite modern PC-based visualization technology, are gaining ground again.

When working with markers, the quality of your handwriting depends not only on how much practice you have had, but above all on proper handling of the markers. Below you will find tips on correct use using as examples the "Edding 800" and "Edding 383" pens:

Always try to write with the edge indicated (below) and not to rotate the marker while writing. As an orientation aid a "sample stroke" is given for each marker in the illustration below, which you can use to check the starting position of the marker.

Fig. 7. Working with felt-tip markers

The simple example below shows you the correct script size for each of the given markers. The important thing here is that the ascenders and descenders be kept short.

By the way: As soon as you succeed in producing the proper script with one marker, you can easily do the same with any other marker, whether a felt-tip marker or a calligraphic pen.

Fig. 8. Script sample   **23**

1.3.2 Design Elements

A visual representation is generally a combination (composition) of different elements.

We call these elements "design elements" of the visualization. Specifically, they are:

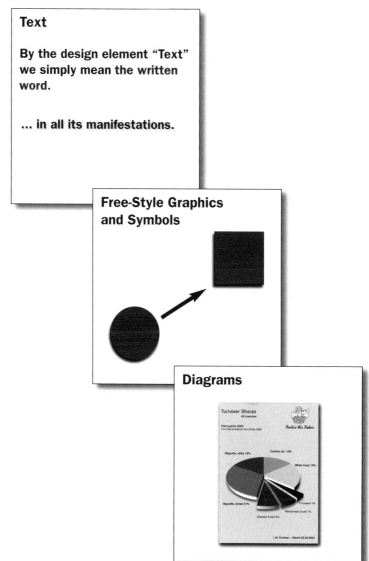

Text

By the design element "Text" we simply mean the written word.

... in all its manifestations.

Free-Style Graphics and Symbols

Diagrams

Fig. 9. Design elements

The Design Element Text

The most common way to visualize information (that is, to make it visible) is to write it down.

As studies have shown, (written) information is most likely to be assimilated by the receiver if the following rules are observed:

A) Keep legibility in mind

- Write legibly!

  When writing by hand use block letters instead of "joined-up" writing. When typing the text, choose simple fonts (such as Helvetica or Arial).

- Adhere to reading conventions!

  Always write from left to right. Begin the representation at the upper left. Use both uppercase and lowercase letters.

B) Observe the four "clarifiers"

- Simplicity

  Use common words. Keep sentences short.

- Structure/Organization

  Use headings and subheadings.
  Form optical blocks.

- Brevity/Conciseness

  Limit what you have to say to the bare essentials. There's an art to omission!

- Additional stimuli

  Utilize color; give examples; use drawings in addition to writing.

The Design Elements Free-Style Graphics and Symbols

The design elements free-style graphics and symbols can be assigned to the clarifier "additional stimuli" (see previous page). They serve to clarify and/or emphasize information. "Dry" topics can be enlivened by these elements.

When pin boards are being used, moderation materials (rectangles, circles, ovals, etc.) make ideal tools for free-style graphics. The diverse colors, shapes, and sizes available make these materials well suited to this use.

When working with computer programs, you usually have many more colors and shapes available than you could ever use. In this case caution is necessary, in order not to be led astray to use "too much of a good thing". Too great a variety of graphical elements can result in the content being eclipsed.

Here are some examples of elements that can be used to design a visualization:

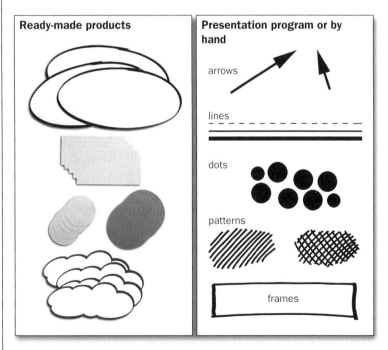

Fig. 10. Elements for free-style graphics

Fig. 11. Standard symbols

Fig. 12. Nonstandard symbols

The Design Element Diagrams

Diagrams are standardized forms of representation for certain subjects.

Examples of this are:

- lists and tables

- graphs

- bar charts

- pie charts

- structure charts/"organigrams"

- flowcharts/arrow diagrams

Depending on the form of the representation, diagrams serve for the comparison of things such as absolute values, developmental processes, or proportions, as well as the illustration of supplies in stock, processes, and structures ...

The most commonly used types of diagram are compiled below, and each is visualized with several examples. This will make it easier for you to find the type of representation that best suits your needs.

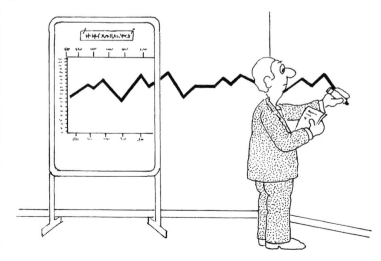

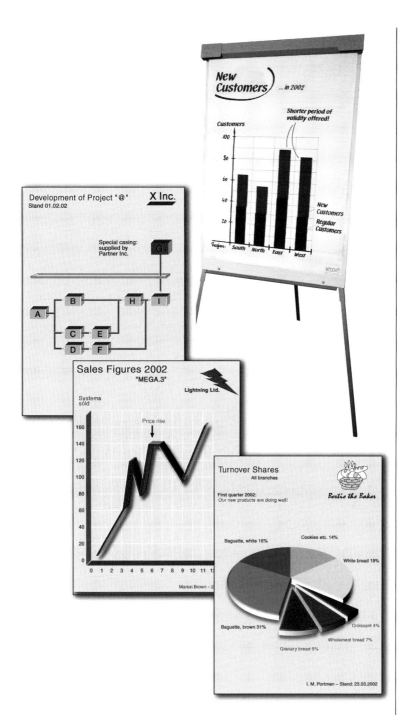

Fig. 13. Diagrams

What?

Lists and Tables

Why?

Lists and tables offer a good way to lend transparency to numbers or values. They are particularly well suited for compiling lists in order to compare ...

... topics
... products
... sources of error
... turnover figures
... warehouse stock figures
...

How?

- The points illustrated by tables must be exactly what you want to present or demonstrate!

- Draw up your table according to the needs at hand (do not simply borrow)!

- Emphasize the most important parts (for instance with a frame)!

- Supply background information (thus enhancing comprehension)!

- (Column) headings must speak for themselves!

- (Column) headings should stand out optically, for instance, use thick separating lines!

- Observe reading conventions (write only horizontally)!

- If there are a large number of lines (and columns) consider numbering them!

- Don't go into too much detail (for instance numbers with three decimal places)!

- Don't forget to give the title and, where applicable, the source!

Examples
Lists and Tables

Customer Quotes

Excerpt from the customer survey 2002

Miller Motors Ltd.

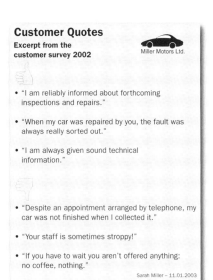

- "I am reliably informed about forthcoming inspections and repairs."

- "When my car was repaired by you, the fault was always really sorted out."

- "I am always given sound technical information."

- "Despite an appointment arranged by telephone, my car was not finished when I collected it."

- "Your staff is sometimes stroppy!"

- "If you have to wait you aren't offered anything: no coffee, nothing."

Sarah Miller – 11.01.2003

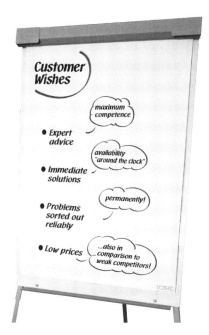

Prices

EXTRAS
Models "2000" & "3000"

Miller Motors Ltd.

Modell / Extras	2000	3000
Metallic paint	1,800.00	1,920.00
Thermal glass	476.00	502.00
Aluminum hubs	2,025.00	2,425.00
Chassis II	1,050.00	1,725.00
Radio with CD	970.00	1,320.00
Sunroof, mech.	876.00	——
Sunroof, elect.	996.00	1,005.00
Air conditioning	2,225.00	2,425.00
ABS	800.00	920.00
ASR	490.00	580.00
Airbags, at back	2,222.00	2,452.00
SOS system (radio)	3,005.00	3,005.00

Sarah Miller – 11.01.2003

Catalog of Important Topics

Miller Motors Ltd.

1. Fluctuation rate

2. Occupational accident figures

3. Absenteeism

4. Defect rate

5. Remachining rate

6. Complaints

7. …

Sarah Miller – 11.01.2003

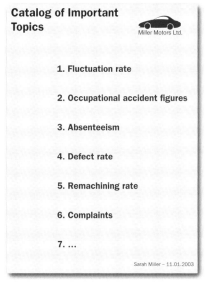

Fig. 14. Lists and tables

31

What?
Graphs

Why?

Graphs are especially well suited for showing the course of developments and for the comparative representation of processes such as …

… turnover development
… development of market shares
… cost development
… remachining rate
… fluctuation rate
…

How?

● The origin of the coordinate system serves as the starting point in graphs!

● The abscissa (horizontal axis) generally serves to represent the course of time!

● The ordinate (vertical axis) is for giving the quantities!

● Remember to scale the axes correctly – proper scaling determines the course of the curve!

● Each axis should be clearly labeled!

● If there is more than one curve, each should be labeled!

● If a graph contains more than one curve, use different line styles (solid, broken,…)!

● Stress the statement to be made, for example by cross-hatching the area between the lines!

● Don't forget to give the title and, where applicable, the source!

Examples
Graphs

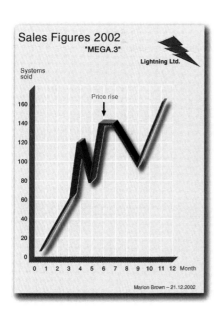

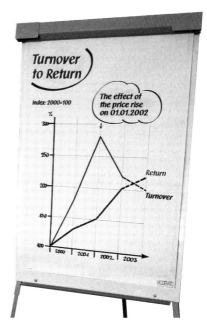

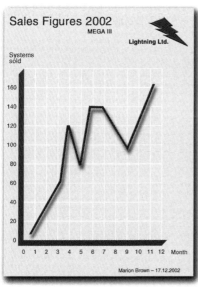

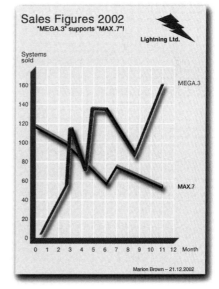

Fig. 15. Graphs   **33**

What?

Bar Charts

Why?

Bar charts are especially well suited for representing comparisons of quantities and for illustrating developments, for example ...

... turnover figures
... warehouse stock
... tax revenues
... remachining work per department or team
... accident figures per month
...

How?

- Decide how the statement you wish to make can be most clearly presented: absolute values, percentages, cumulative values ...!

- Carefully choose the scale of the axes. The representation should clearly reflect the statement you wish to make.

- Use uniform line thickness: As "optical starting points" base lines are thicker than the edge lines of the bars!

- The bars should all be of the same width.

- The space between the bars should not exceed the width of the bars.

- Clearly label the zero lines and indicate the scale you have selected.

- The bars must be labeled.

- Don't forget to give the title and, where applicable, the source!

Examples
Bar Charts

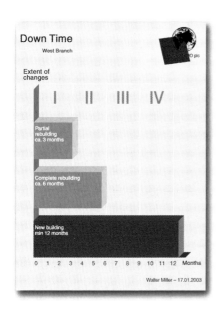

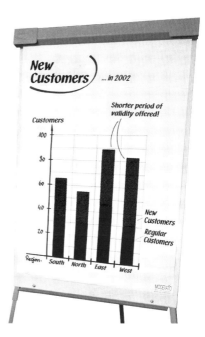

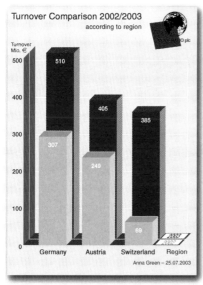

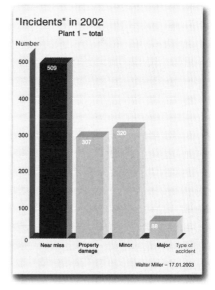

Fig. 16. Bar charts **35**

What?

Pie Charts

Why?

Pie charts always represent the whole and its parts and thus provide a good overall view, for instance of …

… turnover distribution
… market shares
… cost structure
… profit allocation
… distribution of seats (in legislative bodies)
…

How?

- Convert parts of the total quantity to percentages. 360 degrees here correspond to 100 percent!

- Don't show parts that are too small: keep legibility in mind!

- If several small parts are to be represented, group them together to form "collective units."

- The names of the parts can also be written inside each particular wedge of the pie.

- The individual parts must be optically set apart very distinctly, for example with colors and/or cross-hatching.

- If you use colors, choose each color consciously. For example, use the signal color red for delimiting or emphasis.

- Don't forget to give the title and, where applicable, the source.

Examples
Pie Charts

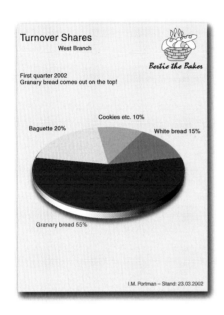

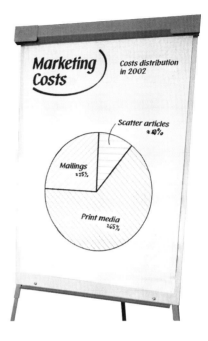

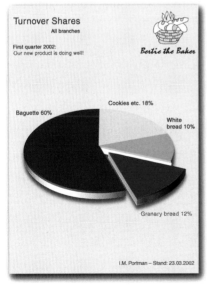

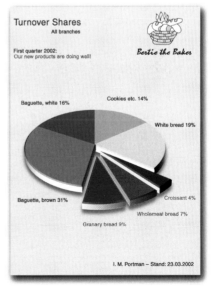

Fig. 17. Pie charts   **37**

What?

Organigrams etc.

Why?

These types of diagram serve for the representation of structures and processes. They are suitable for depicting (complex) relationships such as ...

... the structure of organizations
... the structure of products
... the structure of files
... the flow of production processes
... the flow of events in projects
...

How?

Organigrams/Structure Diagrams

- Use "boxes" to display the distribution of responsibilities and hierarchies in an organization!

- The position of the units (such as boxes) and the line thicknesses, cross-hatching, etc. can illustrate the interrelationships of the units of the organization!

- Classically, a structure diagram becomes more detailed from top to bottom. Alternatively, structures/interrelationships can be depicted starting from the center.

Flowcharts

- Display predefined planned processes and/or processes as they actually occur.

- Use simple symbols such as arrows or standard symbols such as those used in data processing!

- Don't forget to give the title and, where applicable, the source!

Examples
Organigrams etc.

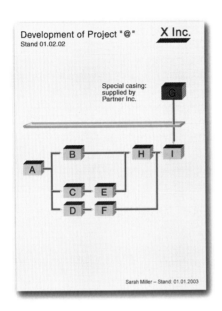

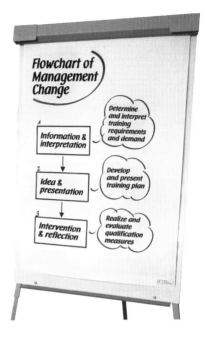

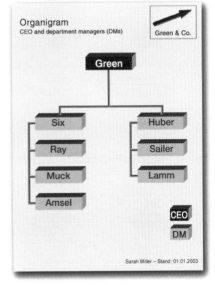

Fig. 18. Organigrams etc   **39**

Decision Matrix

What's best for which purpose?

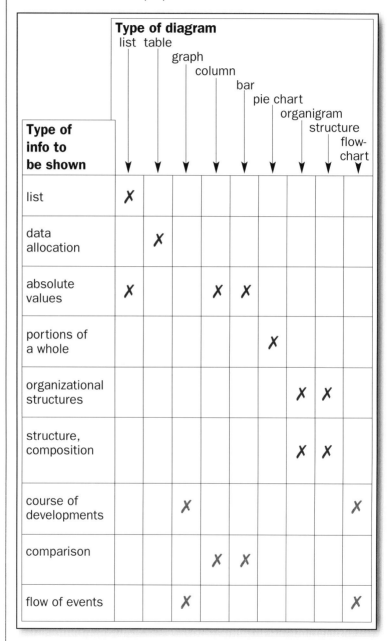

Type of info to be shown	list	table	graph	column	bar	pie chart	organigram	structure	flow-chart
list	X								
data allocation		X							
absolute values	X			X	X				
portions of a whole						X			
organizational structures							X	X	
structure, composition							X	X	
course of developments			X						X
comparison				X	X				
flow of events			X						X

Fig. 19. Decision matrix

1.4 "Composing" a Visualization

The design elements text, free-style graphics and symbols, and diagrams have to be arranged in a ready-to-present form on the media (information carriers) pin-board paper, flip-chart paper, and overhead transparencies or slides, etc. This technique is what we call the composition of a visualization. To achieve as successful an overall presentation as possible you should keep the following points in mind:

- partitioning of the sheet
- logic and arrangement
- colors and shapes

1.4.1 Partitioning the Sheet

To attain a clear (overall) structure in the representation it is first of all necessary to think about partitioning the sheet. For this it is helpful to divide the medium up with a grid, i.e., to divide it into halves or thirds horizontally and/or vertically. You can do this either strictly in your imagination or with thin pencil marks on packing paper and flip-chart paper, and by placing a grid underneath a transparency. The second step is to decide which design elements or parts thereof are to be accommodated in which segments.

Here is an example:

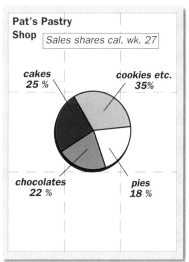

Fig. 20. Rough grid for partitioning the sheet

1.4.2 Arrangement and Logic

For the arrangement of the design elements within the chosen coarse grid there are several basic patterns that you can use as orientation aids:

- symmetry
- alignment
- rhythm
- dynamics

Simple example arrangements – one for each of these "classics" of composition – are given on the next page. The important thing in arranging the design elements is that they are not "randomly" placed in one or other of the patterns, but rather that in their (selection and) arrangement the elements reflect the logical structure of what is to be represented. Thus when planning a visualization you can ask yourself questions such as:

- Do I want to present something as a whole with its component parts? (A question of parts of a whole.)

  For the representation you could use: symmetry/network chart (see pp. 43 and 128).

- Do I want to represent ranks/hierarchical levels? (A question of superior and subordinate ranking.)

  For the representation you could use: alignment/organigram (see pp. 43 and 38f.).

- Do I want to illustrate causes and their effects? (A question of cause and effect.)

  For the representation you could use: dynamics/cause-and-effect diagram (see pp. 43 and 126f.).

- Do I want to compare things with one another? (A question of equality and inequality.)

  For the representation you could use: alignment/ bar chart (see pp. 43 and 34f.)

Examles
Arrangement of the Design Elements

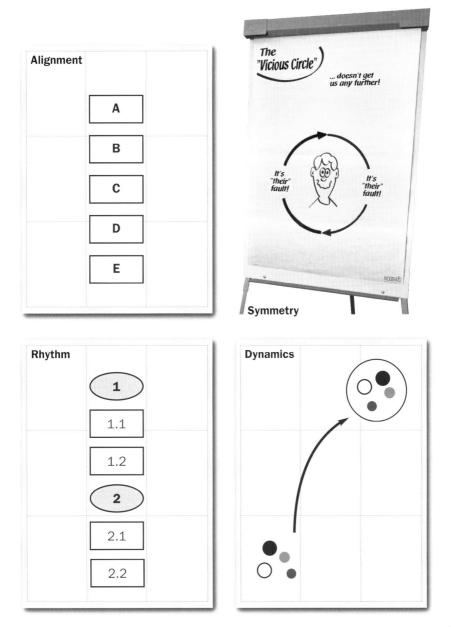

Fig. 21. Arrangement of the design elements   **43**

1.4.3 Colors and Shapes

Aside from the partitioning of the sheet and the arrangement of the elements of the visualization, in the composition of an overall representation the employment of colors and shapes must be carefully planned, because:

colors and shapes have a significance of their own!

Through a meaningful use of colors and shapes:

- vital information is stressed
- correlations are made clear
- cross-references between several representations are produced
- consecutive representations are linked together

Examples
Emphasis in the arrangement

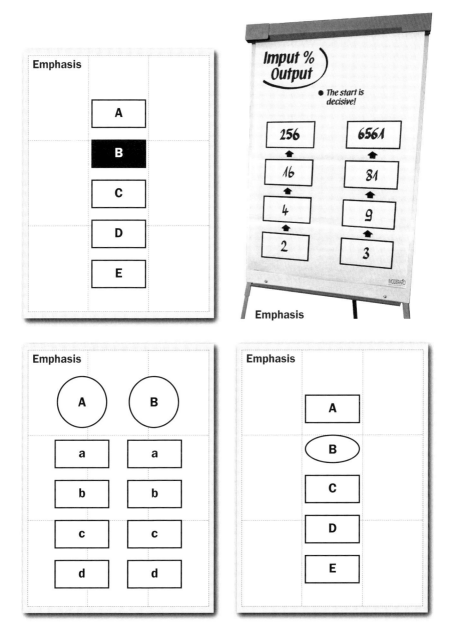

Fig. 22. Emphasis using color and shape   **45**

**And here are just a few general
Tips on Designing Posters:**

- Whenever possible use no more than three
  colors per representation!

- Create blocks; group contextual units (also)
  by displaying them in close proximity to one another!

- Always use the same color and shape for
  related subjects!

- Stress important parts, for instance by using
  red or by using a frame, underlining, or cross-hatching!

- Use empty spaces (also) as a design element;
  leave sufficient areas empty!

- Don't use abbreviations – write everything out!

- Use the stimulating effect of free-style graphics;
  paint a "picture" of your own!

- Whatever you do, avoid perfect representations;
  images that are too "smooth" seem cold
  and create distance!

- Test your visualization(!) by presenting it to friends
  or colleagues, and ask them for their opinions!

To conclude this chapter here is a bit of fundamental advice. Please do not forget that the art of a visualization does not lie in depicting the wealth of information available, but rather just the opposite:

Omission is an art!

In any given case, represent as much as necessary but as little as possible. It isn't the quantity of what is offered that is most effective, but rather its meaningfulness and quality.

2 Presentation

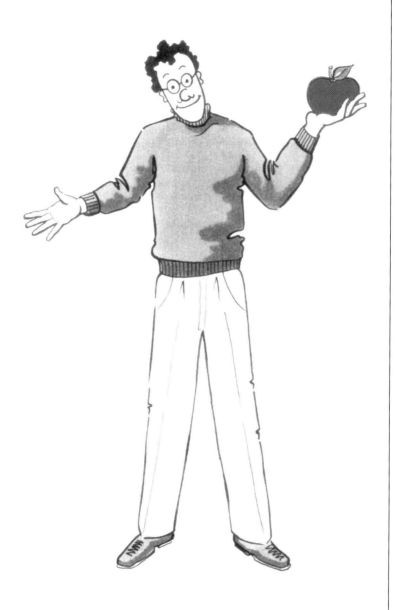

2.1 Presentation – What's the Point?

Good ideas rarely sell themselves on their own. Nowadays, more than ever before, it is necessary to present yourself and your accomplishments, products, etc. in a positive light, i.e., to "show off", to "parade" in front of others.

Aside from little everyday presentations – and the fact is we are constantly presenting something – a presentation is an event at which a presenter introduces a prepared subject to a select circle of participants. The aim of this can be:

- to **inform** colleagues about the latest turnover figures

- to **convince** customers of the benefit of an offer

- to **motivate** a superior to continue project X

"That's all well and good," you'll say, "but just what do I need to pull off a truly effective presentation?"

Since any presentation draws its vitality from the concrete situation at hand, there are no universal rules that guarantee success. Nevertheless, it is highly probable that you will be successful with:

- a carefully thought-out structure of the presentation
- an effective visualization
- a practiced presentation performance

And another thing: a presentation is generally only as good as its preparation – but preparation is a matter of willpower!

> *"A man – or madman should I say? –*
> *Believes: 'The will provides the way.'*
> *'Tis but a matter of degree:*
> *The will alone is fair to see!"*
>
> Eugen Roth

2.2 Preparing a Presentation

As with any planned activity, a presentation begins well ahead of the actual event. It can be divided into three main parts: preparation, conducting the presentation, and evaluation. To begin with we'll deal with the first part, preparing a presentation.

The success of the presentation depends very heavily on its preparation, for at no other point will you be able to exert as much influence on the outcome of the event.

A thorough preparation yields:

- more information, knowledge of details …

- more personal clarity

- the opportunity to target the visualization

- the chance for a smoothly organized course of events

- the preparation of materials required

- ultimately, a more self-confident manner

What does a meaningful preparation entail?

The preparation can be split up into six parts. A presentation has been thoroughly prepared if all parts have been worked on. This refers specifically to the:

- topic
- goal
- target group
- content
- course of events
- organization

Let's take a closer look at these "cornerstones" of preparation.

2.2.1 Preparing for the Topic and Goal

The topic and the goal are often confused with one another: Simply having a topic for your presentation doesn't necessarily mean that its goal is clear as well!

For example, if the topic is "Project ALPHA," it is not yet clear whether …

- … problems in processing,
- … the financial situation, or
- … the prospects for success of the project are to be reported, or whether …
- … a decision is to be prepared or
- … a decision is to be justified, and understanding and support are to be sought …

For you to be able to decide what can or should or even must become the content of the presentation, the goal must be as clearly formulated as possible. Only in this way can you be certain that you do not "miss the point"!

A clearly formulated goal for the above example would be: "Following the presentation the participants will vote to approve additional funds for 'Project ALPHA'." Further planning must now be subordinated to this objective – only information promoting this goal will be used.

2.2.2 Preparing for the Target Group

The term target group means the purposefully selected circle of participants in the presentation. This is the circle of people you wish to and/or have to include in order to achieve your goal. It is also conceivable to look at this the other way around. Who are the participants and to whom will you therefore have to direct the event?

For preparation specifically relating to the participants it helps to ask yourself some further questions, such as:

- Who should or must attend?

  Invite those affected by the subject matter at hand (or their representatives), and also invite persons important for tactical reasons.

- How large should the group be?

  The group should be as large as necessary but as small as possible. If there are to be more than 10 people, look for a partner who can assist you during the presentation.

- Are there things in common that are typical of the target group?

  If the participants do have something in common – e.g., age, gender, occupation, knowledge of the company, prior knowledge of the topic – you must take this into consideration when selecting and preparing the contents of the presentation. If they have nothing in common, you must also take this into account, for instance by presenting more detailed information.

- What interest could the individual participant have in attending the presentation?

  – How does he view the topic?
  – What does she expect from the topic?
  – What does he think of me as the presenter?
  – What does she expect of me?
  – What attitudes do they all have toward each other?

  Knowing the (presumed) attitudes and expectations of the participants helps you on the one hand to avoid neglecting crucial subjects (from the participants' point of view), thus creating frustration, and serves on the other hand to mentally attune you to the situation.

2.2.3 Preparing the Content

Depending on the topic, goal, and target group, the content of the presentation is prepared in three stages, namely:

- gathering material and selecting what is important
- condensing the material
- visualizing the selected contents

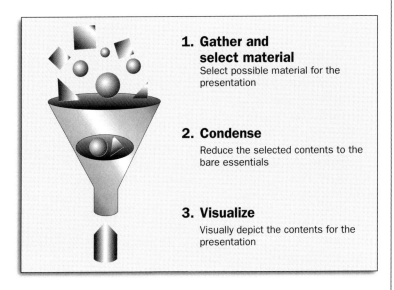

1. Gather and select material
Select possible material for the presentation

2. Condense
Reduce the selected contents to the bare essentials

3. Visualize
Visually depict the contents for the presentation

Fig. 23. Selecting – condensing – visualizing

After you have gathered and organized the possible contents according to the topic of the presentation, you select the relevant information and then condense it to a degree that permits proper handling. When condensing the material you should observe the following points:

- New information (test results, decisions…) take precedence over what is already known.

- Select the information that is most relevant to the objective and meaningful to the target group.

- Limit yourself to the bare essentials!

The information obtained in this way is then sorted into main and subtopics for the presentation and is finally optically laid out in the form of text, free-style graphics, and diagrams on pin boards, flip charts, and/or (overhead) transparencies.

2.2.4 Preparing the Sequence of Events

The presentation itself consists of three parts, the **opening remarks**, the **main body**, and the **conclusion**.

What you have to do to prepare for each individual part is described below. Each section concludes with a checklist of items to remember.

A word of advice: Prepare "crib" notes (such as file cards, approx. 14 – 21 cm or 5 – 8 in., or moderating cards) right from the start, jotting down keywords on all items of your preparation.

A) Preparing the Opening Remarks

At the beginning of any event there will be a word of welcome, either formal or personal, depending on the participants involved. At any rate it makes sense to think beforehand about the appropriate greeting and what you wish to say about yourself (introduction).

The second step in the opening remarks is to indicate

- the occasion
- the topic
- the goal of the event

even if you (could) assume that everyone already knows this. In a third step, reveal the planned "itinerary" so that the participants know "where they are heading." This agenda should contain the following points:

- a main outline of the presentation, including the names of those making the presentation (when more than one are involved)
- a timetable, including the breaks
- announcement of the "catering plan"
- mention of written material, if any, for the participants

The last step of the opening phase is to awaken the participants' interest in the topic to the point at which they can hardly wait to hear more. You can do this by:

- Asking questions

  Questions have the nature of a challenge; they encourage independent thought.

- Establishing personal connections

  Demonstrate what it is that connects the participant with the topic of the presentation.

- Show personal advantages

  Answer the question: What do I as a participant stand to gain by …?

- Be provocative

  Posing an odd, paradox, daring, … thesis can be provocative

Checklist
for the preparation of the opening of the presentation

- **Please check whether you know …**

  - ✓ what you are going to say to officially begin the presentation
  - ✓ what you will say about yourself
  - ✓ how you will link up to the occasion of the presentation
  - ✓ what you wish to say about the occasion, topic, and objective of the event
  - ✓ what items you are going to include in the "itinerary" for the participants
  - ✓ whether you will announce and/or distribute written material to the participants, and if so, how and when
  - ✓ what means you wish to employ to capture the participants' attention and arouse their willingness to listen

B) Preparing the Main Body

In the main body of the presentation you should systematically introduce the topic to your listeners. To do this, sort the contents into main and subordinate items. At this point think about how much material your audience can absorb in the amount of time available, since the maxim that **less is often more** definitely applies here.

It is important that your argumentation be logically structured in a manner that your listeners can follow. In addition to this, you should already think about how you will be able to capture and hold the attention and concentration of the participants. Here are a few ways to do this:

- ask questions (use questions to organize the material)
- offer diversity in the media used
- divide the material into brief presentation segments and allow for breaks
- "visualize" effectively
- use more than one presenter (perhaps a duo)
- use/complete visualizations during the presentation

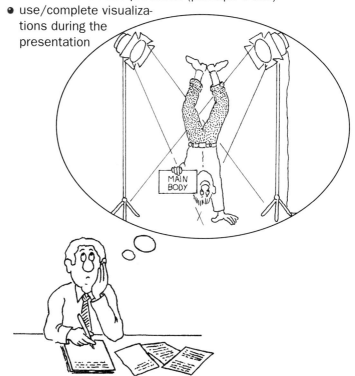

At the end of the main body, give a brief summary of the most important points. Specifically, prepare this part by …

- completely preparing the visualization with appropriate representations (posters, flip charts, transparencies) ahead of time, and/or
- only partly preparing the posters etc. in order to complete them during the presentation, and/or
- considering how you could completely produce the visualization during the course of the event.

Checklist
for the preparation of the main body of the presentation

- **Please check that …**
  - ✓ your material is ordered in a manner that can be easily followed and your arguments are understandable, for instance in a trial run before colleagues;
  - ✓ you have already taken enough time for an effective visualization (see Part 1 – Visualization), for instance by "testing" your visualization before friends and/or colleagues;
  - ✓ you already know what concrete means you will use to hold the participants' attention throughout the presentation.

C) Preparing the Conclusion

The first impression is decisive and the last one sticks. For this reason, the conclusion of the presentation is a vital component of the overall event. If the aim of the event was perhaps to move the participants to take concrete steps, then at this point a clear call to action would be appropriate. In any event thank the participants for coming, then conclude the event with a closing remark. The central points here have – as a rule – already been visualized; you can note the wording of the call to action and of the conclusion on a "cheat sheet."

Checklist
for preparing the conclusion of the presentation

- **Please check …**
  - ✓ what central points the summary at the end should, could, or must contain

✓ what you want to say to conclude the presentation

Depending on what the plans are, a discussion can follow the presentation. This should be every bit as well prepared as the presentation itself.

In preparing for the discussion it is important to consider ...

- what introductory question you will ask
- what opinions could be expressed and by whom
- what arguments and replies could be helpful (if it suits the purpose, collect pro and con arguments)

Checklist
for preparing for the discussion

- **Please check ...**
  ✓ how much time you can and/or want to allocate to a discussion
  ✓ who could relieve you by taking over and leading the discussion
  ✓ what you wish to say to open the discussion and, if applicable, to introduce the leader of the discussion
  ✓ what arguments and/or objections you must expect and how you can respond to them

Remember as leader of the discussion

- to state the goal
- to designate the time frame
- to coordinate requests to speak
- to make sure that more reserved participants also have a chance to speak
- to clarify misunderstandings
- to disarm verbal attacks
- to summarize the results of the discussion
- to close the discussion

Experience has shown that it is helpful to set up a flowchart for the presentation. It determines what is to be done by whom and with what means, and how much time is allotted for this. It can also contain remarks by the presenters.

Here is an **example**:

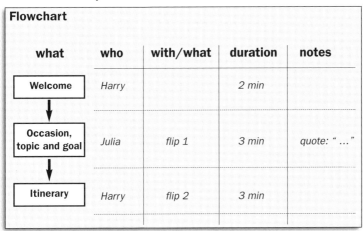

what	who	with/what	duration	notes
Welcome	Harry		2 min	
Occasion, topic and goal	Julia	flip 1	3 min	quote: " ..."
Itinerary	Harry	flip 2	3 min	

Fig. 24. Flowchart for a presentation

For an understandable and lively presentation it is advisable to supplement a good visualization with quotes, vivid comparisons, metaphors, etc. What fits into which part of the timetable and should be used accordingly is noted in the flowchart.

2.2.5 Organizing the Presentation

Good organization alone does not make a successful presentation, but poor organization can condemn a presentation to failure. A thoroughly prepared organization therefore takes the following items into account:

- venue/room
- media
- starting time/duration/breaks
- invitation
- written material for the participants
- personal preparation

Preparation Relating to Venue and Room

First of all you should consider where the event is to take place. If possible a centrally located site and room should be selected to keep the distance to "travel" for each participant as short as possible. If you have decided on a room there are important details to be settled, such as:

- Is the room available for the selected time?
  Who is responsible for reservations?

- Will the room be in an orderly condition at the appointed time? Will it have to be cleaned beforehand?

- Does the room meet requirements in every respect, such as possibilities for darkening the room, temperature, background noise?

- Do signs pointing the way to the room need to be put up? If so, who is responsible for doing this?

One special point is the seating arrangement. It must be precisely organized to prevent unpleasant surprises. The most commonly selected seating arrangements are "horseshoe or semicircle" and "cinema-style seating."

The Horseshoe
The great advantage of the horseshoe or semicircular form lies in the fact that everyone can see everyone else. This makes the atmosphere more personal and facilitates active participation in a discussion. It is possible to work either with or without tables, depending on how the presentation has been set up. Because of the amount of space required, however, this seating arrangement is usually practicable only for smaller groups.

Cinema-Style Seating
The advantage of cinema-style seating is that it saves space and is well suited for presentations before large groups. However, discussions are hampered since not everyone can see everyone else. It can even become necessary for the presenter to be put up on a stage to be (clearly) visible to all participants. It could also be necessary to set up a public address system for acoustical support. This seating arrangement also permits the option of working with or without tables.

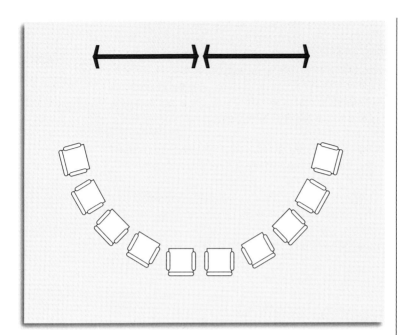

Fig. 25. Horseshoe seating arrangement

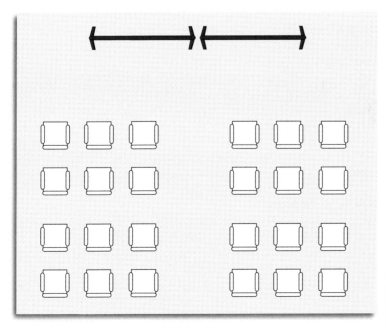

Fig. 26. Cinema-style seating arrangement

Preparing the Media

The organization of the presentation also includes careful planning and selection of the media.

The most frequently used media are pin boards, flip charts, the overhead projector, and PC with a "beamer." You will find a description of these media in **Part 1 – Visualization**. The rules for designing visualizations are also described there. Here are a few more tips on handling:

Pin Boards
Familiarize yourself with your pin boards! Are the boards already at the venue or do they have to be brought in – do you need portable pin boards?

Look at the mechanism! Are the feet securely screwed on or do they fall off when moved? Are they firmly locked in place or do they need to be tightened?

Keep several boards as reserves to fall back on in an emergency. Make certain that you have plenty of pin-board paper, cards, and markers.

Flip Charts
When using flip charts you should check on how the feet are attached, to keep them from loosening up by themselves and collapsing when the stands are moved during the presentation. You should also take a close look at the clip for the flip chart paper.

Does the flip chart stand have side arms for additional sheets or will you need more posting means on the walls or (additional) pin boards?

Overhead Projektor
When using an overhead projector it is imperative that you know how it works, unless you have someone to act as operator.

Don't forget the power supply; if necessary keep an extension lead at hand.

When using an overhead projector, it helps to know exactly …

- … where the device is turned on
- … how to change the transparency (acetate) roll
- … whether the device has a second light bulb and, if so, how to switch over to it
- … if not, how to change the light bulb and where to find the replacement bulb
- … whether sufficient (blank) transparencies and transparency markers (washable/permanent ink) are at hand.

Always check, well ahead of the event …

- whether all technical aids required are present and in working order

- who to turn to about the media, especially if something is defective

- where you can use a copier at short notice if needed

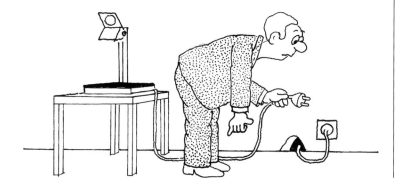

PC, Beamer, etc.

If it all possible:

● Work with your own technical equipment, with which you are familiar!

Technology in the electronic sector alters incredibly quickly, which means that you can only be familiar with some of the technical equipment that you could find at the presentation venue. Therefore avoid questions of compatibility and the inevitable "experiments" that would follow.

● Test your presentation equipment!

Carry out a test with exactly the soft- and hardware constellation that you usually use and which you know works reliably. If necessary, arrange for a test to be carried out at the presentation venue using original files that you have produced (if necessary "dummies") and the equipment that will be available for your presentation.

● Make sure that replacement equipment is available!

It is not unknown that – admittedly only seldom but then certainly at an inconvenient time –

... the hard drive gives up the ghost
... the program crashes and cannot be restarted or, after a successful restart, the presentation will not run
... the fuse in the projector blows
... the bulb in the projector goes

● Familiarize yourself with the equipment!

If one of the above "catastrophes" occurs, you should be in a position – at least in the less severe cases – to help yourself: Where was the fuse? How do you change the light bulb in the projector?...

In the case of (very) small groups you can use the screen of your computer as the "projection surface." If the group is too large for the participants to gather "around the laptop," you can use a conventional cathode ray tube monitor or LCD monitor or a television as the next step up in size.

For large groups, at any rate, you will need a data projector. Make sure that the device has as high a luminous intensity as possible but is also quiet (how noisy is the fan?) and offers a good image resolution.

Another thing: You should have a printed-out set of transparencies for your presentation in your bag to avoid standing there literally "empty handed" if unforeseen technical problems should occur that are not immediately soluble.

CCD Mini Color Camera … and What Else There Is
Without going into details here of all the presentation media that are (currently) available, one thing always holds true: Whatever presentation technology you intend/need to use: **Test your "hardware" thoroughly and arrange for good "crisis management"!**

Preparation Relating to Starting Time and Duration

With regard to time, the following three points should be considered during the preparation:

1. Starting Time

When should the event take place? What time makes most sense with regard to the given objective?

Since virtually everyone experiences a physical and mental low point in the early afternoon, it is advisable not to get into this time of day!

2. Duration

How long should the presentation last?

Next to our health, time is our most precious commodity. No one stays in a positive mood if he has the impression that his time is being wasted! Therefore, the presentation should be as long as necessary and as short as possible.

3. Breaks

How many breaks will there be and when?

Long events should be split up into shorter segments. The first break should take place after 45 minutes at the latest. If refreshments/meals are to be served, think about when, where, and what. "Light" meals are always preferable.

Inviting the Participants

A formal invitation is part and parcel of every presentation. It should contain at least the following five items:

- topic of the presentation
- venue and room (if necessary directions)
- starting time and duration
- presenter(s)
- contact person for inquiries

The participants should **receive** the invitation as early as possible. If the event is important you should request a reply to the invitation!

Preparations Relating to Written Material for Participants

To paraphrase Goethe, "…what you have in black and white you can safely take home with you." In most cases it makes sense to prepare documentation containing the essential points of the presentation for the participants. The important thing in doing this is to know specifically how this material is to be prepared and at what point in the presentation it would be best to distribute it.

For the creation of the documentation please observe the rules for design explained in **Part 1 – Visualization**, and make every effort to provide meaningful, clearly structured material and to orient it toward the participants and the objectives.

Finally, you should decide whether the documents are to be handed out as individual sheets at different times during the presentation or as a "bound copy" at the end. It is generally not advisable to distribute the documentation at the beginning of the presentation, since this would spoil the suspense.

Personal Preparation

Give yourself the "home advantage" by inspecting the rooms, the media, etc. very thoroughly, and take your time in doing so. Take this opportunity to let the presentation come to life in your "mind's eye" (at least) – what/who is to stand where; what is to be picked up from where, and when, etc.

Learn your opening remarks by heart to give yourself more self-confidence.

Make a "cheat sheet." Most suitable is a thin-cardboard card, approx. 14 – 21 cm (5 – 8 in.), listing the principal headings with the pertinent transitions, breaks, etc., all as large and legible (!) keywords. If you need more than one card for this be sure to number them! Prior to major presentations, go through a dress rehearsal, for instance before a group of colleagues and/or a partner.

2.3 Conducting a Presentation

In conducting the presentation what matters is that you implement your preparation in the most effective way. The success of the presentation is directly dependent on you as the presenter, on your ability not only to convince your audience of your factual and professional competence, but also to gain their acceptance of you as a person.

The course of a presentation is divided into three main sections:

- opening
- main body
- conclusion

In the following you will find for each of these sections rules of conduct for the presenter, disruptions that may possibly occur, and ways for the presenter to deal with them.

2.3.1 Tips for the opening

- Pay careful attention to a well-groomed appearance appropriate to the occasion. Nonetheless, you should feel comfortable with the way you are dressed.

- Assume a positive attitude – think of something pleasant.

- Start punctually (9:00 a.m. does not mean 9:07 or 9:15).

- Before you begin to speak make visual contact with your audience. This makes the participants feel that they are being directly spoken to.

- Then, for subsequent eye contact select a "plus man/woman," i.e., someone you know; this affords additional security. However, you should begin to include the entire circle of listeners step by step.

- Begin speaking loudly and clearly (welcome, introduction, topic, occasion and goal, "schedule," transition to the main body).

Possible Disruptions:

- Participant(s) arrive(s) late.

  Don't lose your composure! A brief acknowledgement by eye contact is usually sufficient

- Participant(s) ask(s) questions.

  If questions are asked about the order of events, the topic, or understanding of the content, respond directly to them. If the questions appear to be inappropriate or disruptive, you can defer them until later and alleviate any aggressiveness and reservations that may accompany them by calmly and politely referring them to a later point in time. But beware! Deferred questions must be taken up and answered later. However, not "nonsense".

2.3.2 Tips for the Main Body

- Speak "extempore," that is, just with help from your "cheat sheet."

- Start by introducing the rough outline of this part of the presentation. For example, use a visual representation on a flip chart.

- Use your voice as a tool. Vary the volume, speed, and tone of voice, for example
  - to stress crucial points
  - to emphasize contextual correlations
  - to capture attention

- Form short, easily understood sentences with intentional **pauses**.

- Employ commonly used vocabulary; unless you are speaking before experts, be extremely cautious about using technical jargon.

- Don't try to cover up an accent or dialect, especially when you are among fellow countrymen. The important thing is to be understood. Attune yourself to your listeners.

- Avoid vague or obscuring expressions such as "one," "would say," "might think"…

- Do not consciously suppress gestures.

- If you want to attract attention use more intensive gestures.

- Don't play with markers, pointers, etc. They are there to work with.

- Point directly with your hand, not with objects, unless a pointer is necessary.

- Structure your representation with questions to capture the participants' attention.

Possible Disturbances:

- A slip of the tongue

  Continue speaking and correct yourself to avoid a misunderstanding, but do not apologize.

- Can't think of certain terms

  Describe what you want to say or start over with a brief summary of what has been said up to that point.

- Participants ask questions

  What was said in "Tips for the Opening" holds here, too. Answer comprehension questions, for they demonstrate that the participants are attentive but that possibly your statements are not being equally understood by all. Postpone irrelevant questions with the friendly but firm indication that they will be dealt with at the appropriate time, at the latest during the closing discussion.

- Participants talk among themselves

  Try to regain their attention with eye contact. If the conversation disturbs the presentation, address the source of the disruption and ask the perpetrators something like, "Is your question one that would interest everyone? – Shouldn't we discuss it now?"

- A "bombshell" is dropped

  Don't directly respond to a so-called bombshell (something like "That isn't feasible in practice") since it is not a constructive contribution. You could possibly reply, "I would be glad to discuss this during the break or in the closing discussion."

- There is a technical breakdown

  If possible, simply do without the aid in question, or request a brief interruption and remedy the situation

Here are a few more
Tips for Handling Media:

Pinn Board and Flip Chart

- Be sure that only the visualization you are speaking about at the moment can be seen. Other, irrelevant, representations will only distract the participants.

- Make certain that all those attending have an unobstructed view of the visualization.

- Turn toward the participants while explaining something. Do not talk to the board.

- Stand to one side of the pin board or flip chart and point with the hand nearer the medium.

- Use the visualization as the central theme of your comments.

Overhead Projector

- Do not turn the device on until you need it and turn it off as soon as you are finished with it.

- Do not stand in front of the picture.

- Point, if possible, with the open hand directly at the screen, as if you were standing in front of a pin board.

- If the screen is "over your head", point to the transparency and retain eye contact with the audience.

- If you are pointing to the transparency, use something like a sharp pencil to point with instead of your finger.

- Let the pencil (pointer) lie on the transparency while you are speaking about a particular item.

- Tape the electric lead to the floor (risk of stumbling).

PC & Beamer etc.

- Keep the computer in standby mode so that it is ready for use at any time.

- Use a remote control rather than a mouse to control the presentation so that you do not always have to stand by the computer or keep on wandering to and fro between the PC and the screen.

- If you are not able to stand by the screen and point, install a large mouse pointer that is easily seen and use this to point.

- Avoid placing electric leads where you can trip over them.

In conclusion here are a few
Remarks on Visualization:

When working with an overhead projector, make certain that the **projected** script can be read easily, which means that as a rule you should not use typed text! Here is a tip from an "insider":

If you still want to type the writing on the transparency, do the typing on an A4 or letter-size sheet folded twice and enlarge this original (twice) with a copier so that the final version is A4 or letter size.

A **rule of thumb** for the size of lettering on overhead transparencies is:

Distance from the projection surface	Minimum height of the letters on the transparency
up to 10 m	5 mm
10 – 15 m	10 mm
15 – 20 m	15 mm
20 – 25 m	20 mm
25 – 30 m	25 mm

Fig. 27. Size of lettering on transparencies

73

2.3.3 Tips for the Conclusion

- At the end give a brief summary of the most important points of your presentation – keep it short!

- If you want to appeal to the participants for concrete action, now is the time! Offer active support if the participants are supposed to put something new into action.

- Avoid bland closing remarks such as "That's all for now," or "Let's come to the conclusion"!

- Close with personal thanks to the participants.

- In a final discussion you can now set forth the goals to be achieved and the time frame for doing so, and you can hand over to the discussion leader if there is one other than yourself.

Possible Disturbances

- Unobjective contributions

  As leader of the discussion you should take every contribution seriously and in this way help to maintain objectivity. Ask questions in return to find out what the participant really wants. Be specific! Caution: Even if you feel that you are being personally attacked, keep your objectivity, but don't be "cool."

- A participant elbows his way to the center of attention with his contributions

  Be careful not to focus your attention entirely on one participant alone. Include other participants by asking questions!

2.4 After the Presentation

The presentation does not end when you leave the lecture hall, but rather only after you have conducted a systematic post-presentation evaluation.

This is your chance to learn from concrete experiences and to improve your presentation techniques and behavior. Let the presentation run past your mind's eye again and think about what was successful in the individual phases and what should be different the next time. If you worked in a team then this review should also take place in the team.

For the post-presentation evaluation ask yourself the following questions and jot down the answers as keywords:

- Was the given objective achieved? If not, what went wrong?

- Did the selection of participants fit the occasion?

- Did the presentation meet the requirements of the target group as regards content?

- Did the flow of events work? If not, what changes should have been made?

- Was the opening phase successful? If not, how can it be improved?

- How was the main body – were there critical situations? If so, what were they and how was it possible to master them – what could be done better?

- How did the conclusion turn out – what about the discussion? Is there room for improvement?

- Was everything well organized? If not, what will you have to pay special attention to before the next presentation?

- Did the use of the media run smoothly? Were there any mishaps – what were they and how did you deal with them? What should be done differently in the next presentation?

- How was the relationship, the contact between the presenters? Do you need to work on this?

- How was the contact with the participants? If it was not good, why not? What must be different the next time?

If you are conducting the post-presentation evaluation in a team, it would be helpful to think beforehand about constructive criticism (feedback).

The aim of feedback is for those involved …

>   … to become aware of their behavior
>   … to learn to assess how their behavior appears to others
>   … to see what they trigger off in others

Feedback thus helps to clarify relationships with others and encourages everyone to become better acquainted with and to better understand themselves and the others.

What should Feedback be Like?

If it is to be of any use at all, feedback should meet certain "quality" criteria; it should be:

- descriptive – not judgmental or interpretive
- concrete – not generalizing, not all inclusive
- realistic – not utopian
- immediate – not deferred
- welcome – not forced upon the others

Rules for Giving Feedback?

- Give feedback if it can be helpful

  Feedback is intended to help eliminate communication breakdowns. Do not do without feedback just "to keep the peace." Proper feedback promotes communication.

Avoid making enemies with unqualified feedback. Never employ the technique of feedback to gain personal advantage. Feedback must not be injurious. Feedback does not mean nagging, griping, or insulting. Feedback must be constructive in order to be helpful.

- Give direct feedback/refer to **concrete** details

  Feedback must be understandable; this is easiest if the incident is described as specifically as possible and the time between the incident and the response is as brief as possible. Because of the momentary situation, however, it may be better to postpone the feedback.

- Qualify your statements

  The nature of the feedback should give your partner the chance to accept it. You should therefore intentionally formulate your statement subjectively. Speak of your own observations, impressions, etc. and never those of others.

Rules for Accepting Feedback:

● Whatever you do, let the person speaking finish what he or she has to say

You have no way of knowing what the other person wants to say before he or she has said it. At best you can only guess. Take the time to listen.

● Do not defend yourself/do not set anything straight

Be aware that no one else can ever describe what you are really like, but only how you appear to be to others. This "perception," however, cannot be revised by "setting things straight." But you can learn from this if you want to. Try to understand what the other person means and, if it seems appropriate, ask questions that will provide more insight.

● Thank the other person for the feedback

Be grateful for any feedback (even if it was not given in the proper form). It will help you get to know yourself and your effect on other people and will help you become more competent and self-confident in making an appearance. Moreover, you will always discover something about the biases (expectations) of the other person.

One more thing: Feedback is always merely an offer! You can draw a lesson from it, but you don't have to, since:

> **It's not our purpose in life merely to be**
> **as others would have us be!**

3 Moderation

3.1 Just What is Moderation?

Over the last few decades, new concepts of how to manage people and how people would like to be managed have arisen, regardless of whether this involves members of a workgroup, members of a project group, or participants in a (problem-solving) discussion. As a rule, nowadays the leader is expected not to view himself as the one who dictates what is proper and what is to be done without asking those concerned. Rather he must let the group itself make its own decisions, or at least he must include its members' knowledge, their conceptions, and ideas in his decisions.

One method that helps leaders live up to this expectation has become very popular (and rightfully so!) in recent years: the **moderation method**.

Moderation means a lessening of intensity or extremeness. In the case of the moderation method it stands for:

- a specific basic attitude of the leader (moderator)
- work in accordance with a certain methodology
- use of special aids and materials

The moderation method is used today on the one hand for work in quality circles, "learnshop" work, employee groups – in short, CIP (continuous improvement process) work* – and on the other hand in conducting workshops, taskforce meetings, discussions, etc.

Depending on the given circumstances, a complete moderation cycle can take weeks, or it can be completed within as little as one hour.

---

* See J. W. Seifert and R. Kraus,
Mitarbeiter-Gruppen, GABAL Verlag, Offenbach, Germany 1996

3.2 The Moderator

The moderator is the leader or guide of a group. His style of leading the group is marked by a very specific basic attitude that he "possesses" or strives for: He sees himself as a helper, even a servant of the group. On the basis of this fundamental understanding he does not say what (in his view) is right or wrong, what must or must not be done, but rather he helps the group to work under its own responsibility, i.e., to find its own answers to its questions or solutions to the problems, and wherever applicable to decide on measures that must be taken to solve these problems. He knows that he does not "know it all"!

> *"Let me help you out of the water*
> *before you drown,"*
> *said the monkey amiably*
> *as he set the fish safely in a tree.*

The moderator is a specialist in methodology but not an expert on the subject matter. It is his job to see to it that the group is capable of working and stays that way. He bears the responsibility for the group's ability to work out results, but not for the quality of those results with regard to content. In addition to the pure techniques/methodology of moderation, which will be described in detail in the following sections, the moderator must direct the group process. For this, here are the most important …

Things to Remember

- **Be aware of your impact!**

    All our lives, from cradle to grave, we couldn't stop behaving or "acting" even if we wanted to. Since every action has its impact on others, the moderator cannot choose (any more so than parents, company superiors, etc.) **whether** to have an impact or not, but rather only **what kind**.

    Through this "what kind" of his activity the moderator influences what happens in the group. His behavior has a regulating character. He will set an example for the participants, in either a positive or a negative sense, and will thus affect the atmosphere in the group (and beyond!).

● You are the expert on method, not content!

Even if he possesses factual knowledge of the matter at hand, the moderator has "no opinion of his own" on the topic. He intentionally holds back as far as content is concerned in order to give the members of the group as much freedom as possible for their substantive work (i.e., work related to content).

The moderator has thought out in advance the methods he will use especially for this moderation in working with the participants, in keeping with their objectives (see "Moderation Plan" on page 88). Before each step of the moderation he will explain his methodical course of action to the group and **obtain its consent to proceed**.

The moderator introduces the individual work steps with precisely formulated and visualized questions, and he also steers the group (above all) with questions as the work continues. If the participants direct questions to him that refer to content rather than to the methodical procedure, he simply passes them on directly to the group. The moderator does not comment on or judge contributions made by participants. He makes every effort to remain as neutral as possible.

Moderation is intended to turn merely affected persons into involved ones. For this reason the moderator will always strive to actively include all members of the group in the work at hand.

● Moderate – if possible – in a team of two!

Moderation in a team makes it possible for the moderators to share responsibilities; for example, one could lead the discussion while the other visualizes the contributions made by the participants. This facilitates both the substantive work and the methodical part; it also makes it easier to concentrate on what is happening in the group.

To be able to moderate well, a moderator must always endeavor to understand the contributions of each individual and the content as a whole. In doing so, he "automatically" forms his own opinion, without even wanting to, about the problem and its solution. This is why he is always in danger of "interfering" in the subject matter, losing his neutrality and becoming one of the group (or of the system).

Moderation in a team of two greatly reduces the risk of taking sides with regard to opinions and/or people, since this gives each moderator the chance to keep an eye on the other and if necessary to "rein him in."

When working as a team of moderators it is important for both partners to be thoroughly prepared for the event and for them to agree on how to proceed. In addition, two moderators have a stimulating effect on the group, especially if their personalities complement each other.

In any event you should conduct problematical moderations such as moderation of large groups, controversial topics, "learnshop" work, lean sessions, etc., in a team.

● **There's an exception to every rule!**

Rules are "concentrated experience." They are intended to provide support. When a rule is not helpful under the current circumstances it loses its validity for this particular situation. In other words: Don't cling blindly to the rules of moderation. If necessary, ignore them.

You will find further tips on process control in Section 3.4.4 "Guiding a Moderation Process" (pp. 141ff.)!

3.3 Preparing a Moderation

The success of a moderation depends very heavily on its preparation! The following four aspects should be considered for a thorough job:

- substantive preparation (i.e., preparation with regard to content)
- methodical preparation
- organizational preparation
- personal preparation

Of course in practice it is not always possible to prepare yourself as thoroughly as you would like to. Nevertheless, or maybe even because of this, you should pay as much attention to the preparation as possible in order not to miss any chance of holding a successful event.

As the very first step in a moderation, before beginning with the actual preparatory work, you should ask yourself: Will I be accepted as a moderator by the group that is to be moderated? Some points that could speak against the necessary acceptance could be that you as the moderator, at least from the point of view of the participants, …

- … are not or cannot be sufficiently neutral
- … do not have enough experience to moderate this difficult/ touchy/… topic
- … are not ranked at a level that would encourage willingness to speak openly about … in your presence

If a lack of acceptance must be feared, you should think seriously about what can be (concretely) done beforehand to ensure acceptance. For example, in case of doubt a brief conversation with (the) participants could be conducted. If necessary, you could turn down the job!

One alternative is always an external moderator who has corresponding experience and is neutral per se. The more "touchy" the event, the more seriously should this possibility be considered.

Only after these questions have been thought over very carefully should the actual preparatory work begin. Only then should you start thinking about content, methods, and organization of the event and about your own personal preparation.

3.3.1 Preparation Related to Content

To be sure, the moderator is neutral and has "no opinion" on the contents of the moderation; however, he does lead the group meeting (above all) with questions. But everyone knows that you can only ask questions if you already know something. For this reason it is absolutely necessary for the moderator to know something about the subject matter on which the group will be working. The moderator does not have to be – indeed he should not be – an expert on content. However, he must be capable of "thinking his way into" the subject at hand. Thus it can be helpful, even necessary, for the moderator to take a look ahead of time at the content/topics to be dealt with.

3.3.2 Clarifying the Objective

When planning a moderation, the very least the moderator must do is to define the overall theme and the overall/general objective, in order for a suitable methodical concept to be drafted on this basis.

> *"If I do not know where I want to go, it should come as no surprise if I arrive somewhere I do not want to be!"*

If single topics have already been set (such as items on the agenda for a discussion), the aim of each of the different topics must be defined.

3.3.3 Preparing for the Participants

The central "element" of a moderation are the participants who come together to handle topics affecting them in one way or another. The meeting will thus be shaped by the participants. For the preparation of the event it is therefore important for you to know who is going to be there and to ask yourself …

- How is the group made up? Who is taking part?
- What interest does each individual have in attending?
- What is his or her attitude toward the topic?
- What is his or her attitude toward me as moderator?
- What problems, what conflicts could occur?
- What experience have the participants had with the method?
- What prior information do they have?

It may then be necessary to figure out suitable methodical steps for you to be as well prepared for the participants as possible and to "get on their wavelength." For instance, you could perhaps ...

... allow for an especially long introductory phase if the group members have had no previous experience with the moderation method and you have reasons to fear that this could cause inhibitions or even rejection.

... work out a suggestion to introduce "rules of the game of working together" if the topic is especially controversial for the participants.

3.3.4 Methodological Preparation

Setting up a Moderation Plan

Any advance planning of a moderation means "planning the unplannable," i.e., the moderator cannot know in advance what will happen in the group. But since moderation is a procedure that is heavily method oriented, the work in the group stands and falls with the methodology. It is therefore especially important to be thoroughly prepared methodically.

This means that for every moderation step the moderator precisely plans what the aim of this segment is, what methods he wants to employ to achieve this aim, and what material aids he needs for this. He will estimate the amount of time required and, if he has a co-moderator, he will agree with him on who will assume which tasks.

If individual topics are already known, a possible procedure for each topic should be prepared. For important/problematical/... sessions it is even advisable to work out alternatives and keep them in reserve.

A good aid for the methodical planning of a moderation is a "moderation plan" such as that shown in Fig. 28 (p. 88).

If advance planning is not possible, the moderation must be planned simultaneously, that is, during the course of the group work, possibly together with the participants!

Preparing the Visualization(s)

Aside from the questioning technique, visualization is the central technique of moderation. As a rule, something must be done in preparation for this. The moderator decides what posters, flip charts, cards, etc. he can or must prepare in advance in keeping with the selected procedure; he notes this in his moderation plan and prepares the necessary visualizations.

Moderation Plan for ...

Step	Aim	Method	Aids	Time	Moderator
entire modera-tion	to decide on first measures for shortening our delivery times	entire moderation cycle	1 moderation case 5 pin boards 1 flip chart + visualizations	ca. $3^1/_2$ hrs.	Team: A + B
1 intro-duction	opening good working atmosphere leading up to	single-dot question	prepared poster - visualized grid - visualized question	15 min	A opens B presents question ...
2 gathering	to know what aspects the group wants to discuss	card question	prepared poster - visualized question - extra boards	20 min	B leads A writes
3 selecting	to set the topic the group wants to deal with first	multi-dot question	prepared poster - topic store	10 min	A moderates multi-dot question
4 handling	problem analysis & to find starting points for solving the problems	on-the-spot decision: problem-analysis scheme or cause-effect diagram	prepared poster - problem-analysis scheme and cause-effect diagram	90 min	B leads A writes
5 planning	catalog of measures for improving the situation	catalog of measures	prepared poster - chart of measures	60 min	A leads B writes
6 conclusion	conclusion of the group work	mood barometer	prepared poster - barometer - visualized question	20 min	B summarizes A closes

Fig. 28. Example of a moderation plan

3.3.5 Organizational Preparation

The extent of the organizational preparation to be done depends on the group, the topic, the objective, the procedure selected, and the length of the meeting. In making your preparations you must answer the following questions:

● **Starting time/duration**

  ✓ When should the meeting take place?
  ✓ How long should it last?
  ✓ How many breaks should there be and when?

● **Venue and room**

  ✓ Where should the meeting take place (here/elsewhere)?
  ✓ How many rooms will be needed (plenum and group session rooms)?
  ✓ How large must the rooms be?
  ✓ Are the necessary media and aids available or will they have to be brought in?
  ✓ Have the rooms and if necessary the media been reserved and prepared for the appointed time (chairs, tables for material, media …)?
  ✓ Have arrangements for refreshments been made?
  ✓ What leisure activities are available (for participants staying overnight)?

● **Seating arrangement**

Fig. 29. Seating arrangement

The typical seating arrangement for a moderation is a semicircle with no tables, as shown in Fig. 29. The advantage of this is that each person can see the others; this encourages active participation in what is happening in the group. Furthermore, it is easily possible for each member of the group to step to the front, for instance to place a dot on the board. There is usually no need for the members of the group to take their own notes, since simultaneous minutes are generally taken.

- **Media**

  ✓ What media will be needed?
  ✓ How many pin boards? (Rule of thumb: one pin board for every two participants and two for the moderator.)
  ✓ How many flip charts? (One flip chart per room is usually enough.)
  ✓ Is there an adequate supply of packing paper and flip-chart sheets?
  ✓ What moderation material will be needed (cards, markers …)?
  ✓ Are additional media necessary (overhead projector, slide or film projector, video system …), perhaps for an information phase?
  ✓ Can the room in question be darkened?
  ✓ How about electric outlets? Are extension leads available?

In this connection it is important always to think of an ample supply of spare material. Nothing is more embarrassing than when an event cannot proceed as planned because packing paper or flip-chart sheets are missing, no replacement bulbs for the overhead projector can be found, or there are not enough pins for the pin boards.

- **Invitation**

  The participants should be invited to the event as early as possible. The invitation should at least contain information about:

  – starting time/duration
  – venue/room
  – topic/objective

- participants
- moderator(s)
- initiator/host

Since the only persons invited to a moderated group session are those who are affected by the topic and are (therefore) important for the event, as a rule it makes sense to agree on a date ahead of time by telephone.

3.3.6 Personal Preparation

The main point of personal preparation is to make certain, much like an athlete, that your full mental and physical potential is at your disposal at the appointed time and that you are able to exploit it. To be more specific, you should think about the following points:

● **Physical and mental fitness**

The more important the moderation, the more important it is to pay attention to physical fitness. As a rule you can increase your powers of concentration by eating lightly and not drinking alcoholic beverages, planning adequate breaks and not spending every free minute with the participants, so that you can have some time in between for reflection and regeneration. It can be extremely helpful in the planning phase, for instance on the basis of the moderation plan (see p. 88), to allow the events to run their course before your mind's eye, to feel your way into the situation, to tune in and "make adjustments" at places where you are not certain that you are adequately prepared.

● **Home advantage**

If at all possible, you should familiarize yourself with the locality beforehand and create a "home advantage" for yourself in this way. Every venue has its own peculiarities. It encourages or inhibits a good working atmosphere. Getting to know the premises early gives you a chance to make the best of the given situation.

3.4 Conducting a Moderation

3.4.1 The Course of a Moderation

A moderation is divided up into several segments. The classic course of events is composed of six steps:

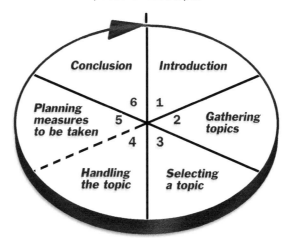

Fig. 30. Steps of a moderation cycle

Step 1: "Introduction"
The purpose of this first step in the moderation is to open the session, create a positive working climate, and provide orientation for working together.

Possible procedure:

● Open the session

Objectives:
to officially start the work in the group;
to agree on a timetable, at least on "key points;"
if necessary to get to know one another (the participants and the moderator);
to become familiar with the surroundings (room, media);
to create a positive working atmosphere.

- Clarify expectations

  Objectives:
  to get to know the expectations of the participants
  and of the moderator;
  to discuss possibly existing reservations;
  to agree on rules for working together.

- Coordinate/formulate the goal(s)

  Objectives:
  to provide orientation with regard to content;
  to coordinate and/or define the goal(s) of working together.

- Coordinate/define the methodology

  Objective:
  to introduce the planned procedure to the participants and coordinate it with them, or to set up a suitable procedure with them.

- Decide how the minutes should be taken

  Objective:
  to agree on the form in which the minutes should be taken, such as simultaneous minutes, and who will take them.

Step 2: "Gathering Topics"
Gathering the topics is the first substantive work step. The purpose of this is to set forth the topics that could be treated or that are specifically to be dealt with. The development of this step could look like this:

  Possible procedure:

- Formulate a precise, goal-oriented question and visualize the question on the pin board

  Objectives:
  to concentrate the participants' thoughts on
  the common goals;
  to create a starting point for the substantive
  work together.

● Distribute moderation cards to the participants and then call on them to respond to the question in writing

Objectives:
to collect ideas on the question asked;
to include all participants and their topic requests.

● Collect in the cards, arrange and structure them on the pin board

Objectives:
to gain perspective, to create transparency;
to find substantive focal points

Step 3: "Selecting a Topic"
The purpose of this is to determine which topic is to be handled or the order in which the topics are to be handled, that is, to set priorities.

Possible procedure:

● Set up a "topic store" (see p. 114f.), i.e., a listing of the topics found, on the pin board or flip chart

Objectives:
to have the key words available "at a glance;"
to facilitate further (methodical) processing.

● Formulate a goal-oriented question and visualize it on the pin board

Objectives:
to concentrate the participants' thoughts on the goal of this moderation step;
to prompt selection of personally favored topics

● Have the topics weighted by "dots," i.e., call on the participants to cast their vote using adhesive dots

Objective:
to give the topics collected the ranking desired by the participants.

Step 4: "Handling the Topic"
In this work step the topics are handled in the order of their importance as determined by the group.

The objectives can be:

- to gather/exchange information
- to analyze/solve problems
- to prepare for a decision
- to make a decision

Possible procedure:

- Suggest a suitable methodology for handling the particular topic, such as working with a problem-analysis scheme.

  Objective:
  to guarantee as efficient a treatment of the topic as possible.

- Handle the topic using the selected methodology

  Objectives:
  to ensure as concrete a treatment of the topic as possible; to focus the participants' attention on the goals of the work and on the chosen methodical procedure.

Step 5: "Planning Measures to be Taken"
In this step the measures to be taken as a result of the treatment of the topic are determined.

Possible procedure:

- Draw a matrix of the plan of action on the pin board

  Objective:
  to create a structure for future work.

- Enter the activities considered to be necessary in the matrix

Objective:
to document the measures slated for concrete implementation, so that everyone can see them

- Assign responsibilities and deadlines for every measure to be taken and, if necessary, agree on controls.

Objective:
to commit the participants to concrete action and to fix clear deadlines to guarantee that the measures are in fact implemented

Step 6: "Conclusion"
The substantive work has now been finished. This is the opportunity to reflect on the group process, i.e., to discuss the following questions together:

- Have my expectations been fulfilled?
- Do I feel that the work has been effective?
- Am I satisfied with the results?
- Did I feel comfortable with the group?

Reflections of this nature can also make sense at an earlier point in time, namely if …

… participants voice dissatisfaction;
… the substantive work becomes bogged down;
… the work has been interrupted by a longer than
usual break.

The moderator ends the session by thanking the participants.

Remark: The possible flow of events of a moderation outlined here serves to illustrate the phases in the course of a moderation process; the methods pertaining to this are described in the section on methods (Section 3.4.3).

Moderation Cycle (Example)

1. Introduction / Orientation

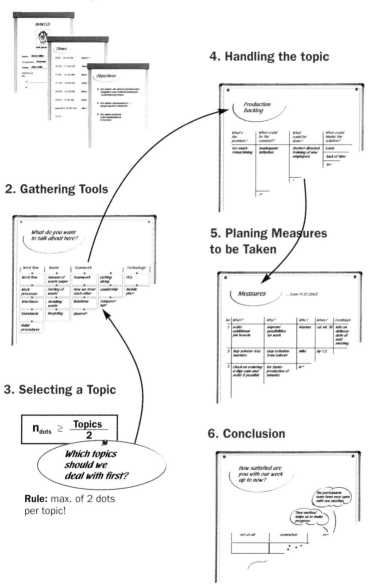

2. Gathering Tools

3. Selecting a Topic

$$n_{dots} \geq \frac{Topics}{2}$$

Which topics should we deal with first?

Rule: max. of 2 dots per topic!

4. Handling the topic

5. Planing Measures to be Taken

6. Conclusion

Fig. 31. Example of a moderation cycle

3.4.2 Moderation Aids

There is a standard set of moderation aids, which can be purchased at any specialized retailers. Keeping the materials in a so-called "moderator's case" has proved to be helpful in moderation practice.

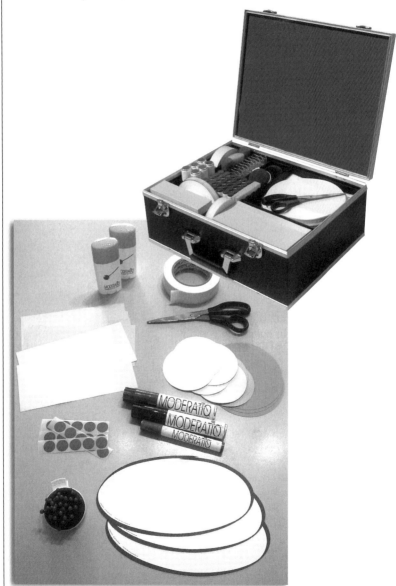

Fig. 32. Moderation aids

The media used in a moderation, namely flip charts and pin boards, are described in **Part 1 – Visualization**.

Fig. 33. Moderation media

3.4.3 Moderation Methods

The moderator is a specialist in methods. It is his job to ensure that the group is capable of work and stays that way. He bears the responsibility for the group's ability to produce results.

The following pages contain a series of moderation methods and/or procedures that have been put to the test and frequently used in practice. For better clarity each one is assigned to the most appropriate step in the moderation cycle and is illustrated with an example.

To remind you that, ideally, two moderators should always work with a group, in the following "catalog of methods" we will speak of **moderators**.

We have put the **questioning technique** at the head of the catalog of methods, as this, in addition to visualization, is the central method of moderation. The "art of asking questions," so to speak, is part of the moderator's basic equipment.

The Question in a Moderation

The moderator, when working as a moderator, is never simultaneously an expert on the subject matter of the group work. He must therefore carry out his duties not from a position of issuing statements or providing answers, but rather from one of asking questions.

Questions make it possible:

- to include all participants;
- to disclose the knowledge of the members of the group;
- to coordinate work steps;
- to cast a light on moods;
- to establish a group rapport;
- …

It is fundamental that the moderator masters the most important types of questions in order that he can …

- ask good questions himself;
- confidently handle questions from the group.

A question is always composed of two parts: the content and the form. The most important interrogative forms are

- the open question
- the closed question
- the alternative question
- the rhetorical question
- the suggestive question
- the counter question
- the returned question

The open question
The open question permits different answers. The person asked can freely formulate his or her answer. The question begins with an interrogative (who, what, how, which, why …). The open question is the major type of question in a moderation.

Example:
"What topics should we deal with in today's group session?"

The closed question
These questions can only be answered with yes or no. This type of question should not be used often for substantive work in the moderation . However, it is very helpful in structuring the work.

Example:
"Can we move on to the next step now?"

The alternative question
This type of question is appropriate if a decision between two alternatives is to be made. The use of this type of question in a moderation needs to be carefully considered because it may possibly split the group into two camps.

Example:
"Shall we continue working on this item or move on to the next point?"

The rhetorical question

Rhetorical questions are often asked to nip contrary opinions in the bud. The question actually answers itself as a matter of "common sense." This type of question is unsuitable for a moderation, since it undermines the desired atmosphere of openness.

Example:
"Do we want to go on with this topic forever?"

The suggestive question

This is a manipulative question designed to move those being questioned to concur. It is considered a "trick" question and is usually held against whoever asks it – also in a moderation.

Example:
"Surely you share my opinion that we have now spent more than enough time on this topic?"

The counter question

Every question has the nature of a challenge – it calls for a response. The best way to escape this pressure is to reflect it, i.e., to answer the question with another question. However, this can be irritating, especially if it is used repeatedly.

Example:
Question: *"When are we finally going on to the next item?"*
Counterquestion: *"Why do you ask?"*

The returned question

This is not a question in its own right, but rather a specific manner of dealing with questions. It plays an important part in moderation. A question directed towards content is passed on (or back) to the entire group, since, after all, the group bears the responsibility for producing results as far as the content is concerned.

Example:
Question to the moderator: *"Shouldn't we speak to the director about this?"* – *"What do the others think?"* asks the moderator and in this way hands the question back to the group.

Catalog of Methods

In the field of moderation concrete procedures relating to one moderation step are referred to as methods. Fundamentally, anything is allowed as a method if it works, provided that it is in keeping with the "spirit of moderation."

In the following we describe (the) methods of moderation on the basis of examples. In each instance tips are given on:

   …the field of application (why?)
   …the procedure (how?)
   …the moderation step within the moderation cycle in which
      the particular method can be applied (when?)

What?

"Getting-to-Know-You Matrix"

Why?

To get (better) acquainted, especially if the participants don't know each other very well.

Advantage:
Because it doesn't take up much time, the getting-to-know-you matrix is also suitable for shorter meetings.

Disadvantage:
The participants do not get to talk to each other very much.

How?

The moderators present to the group a getting-to-know-you matrix already visualized on the pin board. The headings are directed towards the target group and the objective of the event. There should always be a column addressed to the personal/emotional sphere of the participants. This makes it clear from the start that the meeting is not about the subject matter alone, but rather that each participant is also important as a person.

The participants fill in the matrix with the information about themselves either before the meeting officially begins – something which relieves the tension of the first moments – or during the introductory round at the pin board. The moderators also add their data.

When

In Step 1: "Introduction""

Introduction

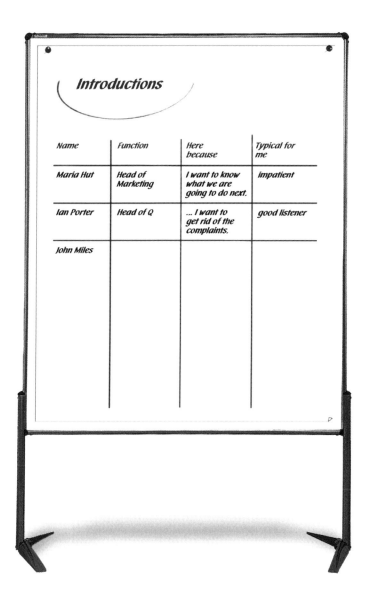

Name	Function	Here because	Typical for me
Maria Hut	*Head of Marketing*	*I want to know what we are going to do next.*	*impatient*
Ian Porter	*Head of Q*	*... I want to get rid of the complaints.*	*good listener*
John Miles			

Fig. 34. Getting-to-know-you matrix

What?

"Wanted" Poster

Why?

To get acquainted and to "warm up," especially if the participants don't know each other very well or even at all, and if the meeting will last several days.

Advantage:
The participants have the opportunity to talk to each other. This encourages a trusting and open atmosphere.

Disadvantage:
Takes up a lot of time.

How?

Alternative 1: Individual introduction

The moderators show the group a prepared questionnaire. The questions are specifically aimed at the target group. It is important for these questions to refer not only to the work to be done. Each participant takes a flip-chart sheet and designs his or her own personal "wanted" poster. The moderators do the same. Afterwards, each person uses the wanted poster to introduce himself or herself. The participants have the opportunity to ask additional questions.

Alternative 2: Interview in pairs

The entire group is divided up into teams of two. Make sure that the partners in a team are strangers to each other if possible. The partners in the teams now interview each other (for about 15 minutes), using the prepared questions, and visualize the answers. Then the participants introduce themselves or each other to the assembled group.

When

In Step 1: "Introduction"

Introduction

WANTED

Self-portrait

Name: _____

Occupation: _____

Hobby: _____

Stations in
life:

   A) _____

   B) _____

   C) _____

Fig. 35. "Wanted" poster

What?

"Survey of Expectations"

Why?

The participants and moderators get to know the expectations and any reservations or anxiety the others may have with regard to working together, and they can prepare themselves accordingly. Any tensions are reduced in this way or become handleable, so that they can be voiced. Trust and openness are thus promoted.

If it seems appropriate the participants can agree on rules ("rules of the game") in which they set forth how they wish to interact (see Section 3.4.4 "Guiding a Moderation Process," pp. 141ff.).

How?

Alternative 1: Complete the sentence

The moderators put up a prepared poster with a visualized beginning of a sentence and call on the participants to complete this sentence. Either the moderators (as the participants call out their responses) or the participants themselves visualize their contributions on the board.

Alternative 2: Single-dot question

The moderators put up a poster depicting a scale for assessing personal expectations and call on the participants to cast their vote using an adhesive dot (see "Single-dot question," pp. 116f.).

When?

In Step 1: "Introduction"

Introduction

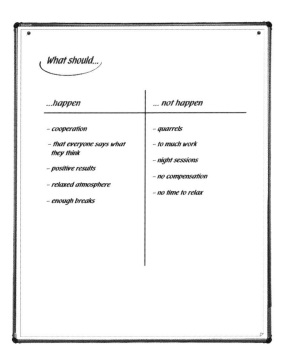

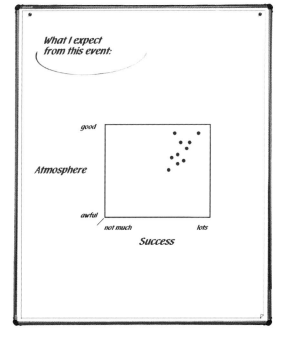

Fig. 36. Survey of expectations

What?

"Called-Out Responses"

Why?

The method of called-out responses can be used in much the same way as the card question (see pp. 112f.) to gather topics, questions, ideas ....

Advantage:
Requires little time. "Brainstorming effect" through chains of association.

Disadvantages:
The volunteered responses can only be (re-)organized with difficulty. They are not anonymous. It is most difficult to treat all participants equally; not everyone is involved to the same extent.

How?

The moderators pose a question that has already been visualized on a flip chart or pin board and ask the group to respond. The participants call out their answers to the moderators. One moderator guides the process while the other writes down the replies for all to see.

When?

Mainly in Step 2: "Gathering topics"
According to the situation, in any moderation step

What do we have to do/discuss today?

- Handling the new
  flexitime arrangement

- Autonomy of the teams

- Replacement for Ms. Pink

- Interim jobs

- Standard equipment/
  equipment standards

- Settlement of
  traveling expenses

Fig. 37. Called-out responses

What?

"Card Question"

Why?

The card question is the method of choice for gathering topics, questions, ideas, suggestions for solutions, etc.

Advantages:
Every participant is involved. All answers are equally important; there are no hierarchical or other differences. The responses can be rearranged at any time.

Disadvantages:
Very time-consuming. With large groups and/or a large number of answers it can become confusing. However, this disadvantage can be alleviated to some extent, since it is possible to limit the number of cards.

How?

The moderators ask the group a question that has been visualized on a pin board. The participants are to write down their answers. For this purpose the moderators hand out moderation cards. They have a uniform color to prevent single cards from standing out due to their color alone (note: colors and shapes have a significance of their own!).

The participants are now asked to write their answers to the question on the cards. In doing so, they should ...

> ... write with felt-tip pens
> ... print
> ... use large, clear writing and a maximum of three lines per
>   card so that everyone can read them later on when they are
>   posted on the pin board
> ... include no more than one thought per card

The next step is now to collect in the cards. In doing this be careful to collect them face down. This is important because open card questioning is supposed to be as anonymous as possible. Finally, the cards are pinned to the pin board.

The following division of labor of the moderators is sensible: While one shows a card to the group and reads it aloud, the other prepares the drawing pins and pins the card to the board.

For each subsequent card the moderator asks the group whether this card can be grouped with those already on display or if it forms a new category of meaning and should therefore be pinned up beside the others instead of below them. This process is complete when all the cards are pinned on the board.

Finally, the group again examines the classification of the cards and provides each group of cards (categories of meaning) with an appropriate heading.

When?

Mainly in Step 2: "Gathering Topics"
According to the situation, in any moderation step

Gathering

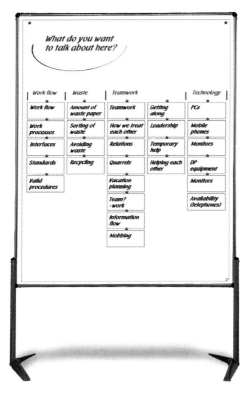

Fig. 38. Card question

What?

"Topic Store"

Why?

The topic store makes it easier to keep track of the focal points found and lays the foundation for further work.

Advantage:
Provides a good overview of the situation.

Disadvantage:
An additional work step is required to add the topics to the topic store.

How?

Working together with the group, the moderators list the topics that are to be (further) treated. They have been determined in advance or worked out by the group by a card question or called-out responses.

The topics are then dealt with in the order in which they appear. As an alternative, they can be evaluated with dots to set priorities (for more on this see "Multi-dot question" on p. 118).

When?

At the end of step 2: "Gathering topics"
At the beginning of step 3: "Selecting a topic"

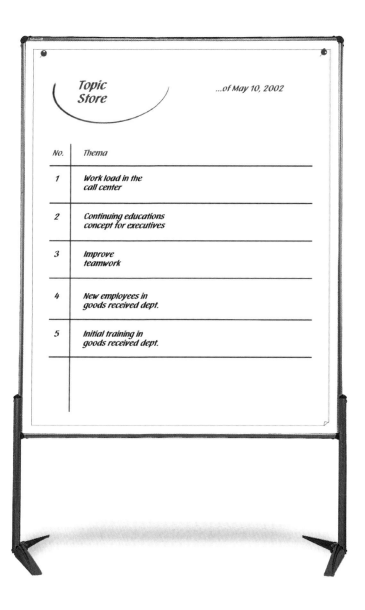

No.	Thema
1	Work load in the call center
2	Continuing educations concept for executives
3	Improve teamwork
4	New employees in goods received dept.
5	Initial training in goods received dept.

Topic Store ...of May 10, 2002

Fig. 39. Topic store

What?

"Single-Dot Question"

Why?

A single-dot question is used to create transparency and to make decisions. For example, it is a good tool for making it clear at the point of entry into a topic how difficult the group members consider treatment of the topic to be, or to provide a clear picture of their level of information on the subject.

How?

The moderators call on the members of the group to answer a previously formulated and visualized question by sticking a dot on the appropriate place. For this purpose a sliding scale such as "easy – difficult"/"good – bad" or an assessment scale with categories such as "easy – fairly easy – fairly difficult – difficult" is provided. The participants cast their votes by sticking an adhesive dot to the appropriate place on this chart.

In any event, the result is discussed immediately afterwards.

Alternative 1:

The moderators ask the group to comment on the results.

Alternative 2:

The moderators ask each participant to say where he or she placed a dot and to briefly explain why.

When?

Any moderation step, according to the situation;
but especially in Step 1: "Introduction"

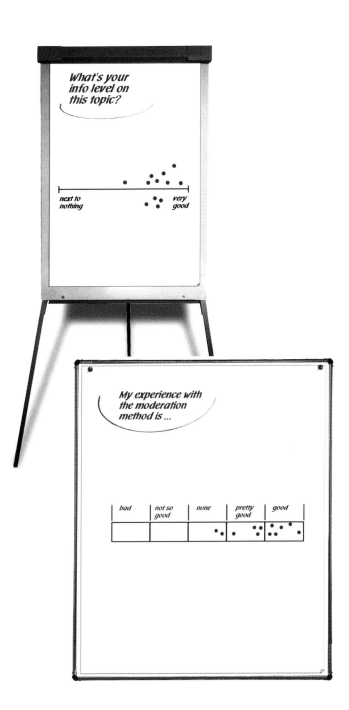

Fig. 40. Single-dot questions

What?

"Multi-Dot Question"

Why?

A multi-dot question in a moderation session serves as a substitute for a vote. It lends itself well to making decisions and setting priorities.

How?

The moderators call on the participants to respond to a previously formulated and visualized question by sticking several dots on the chart. A number of choices must be provided for this, such as headings taken from the collection of topics listed in the topic store.

Rule: The number of adhesive dots corresponds to the number of alternatives divided by two, rounded off to a whole number if necessary.

Each participant sticks a maximum of two dots on the pin board for each choice of topic for which he or she has decided.

When?

Step 3: "Selecting a topic"

Selecting

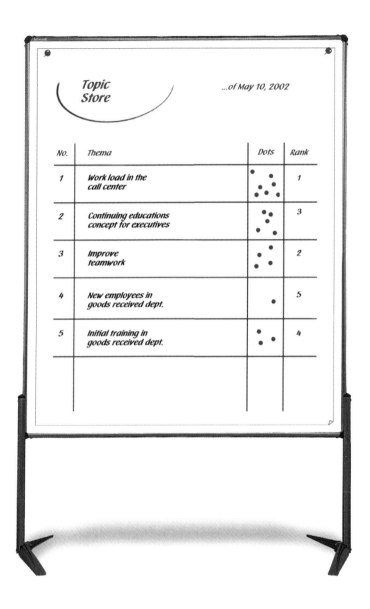

No.	Thema	Dots	Rank
1	Work load in the call center		1
2	Continuing educations concept for executives		3
3	Improve teamwork		2
4	New employees in goods received dept.		5
5	Initial training in goods received dept.		4

Topic Store ...of May 10, 2002

Fig. 41. Multi-dot question

What?

"Two-Part Board"

Why?

Like the "four-part board" (see pp. 122f.), this method is especially well suited for treatment of a topic in small groups. It serves to roughly clarify a (sub-)topic, to expose possible conflicts, to develop first approaches to finding a solution, ...

Advantage:
The "two-part board" provides a clear structure and enables a rapid preliminary treatment of a topic. It is very easy to implement.

Disadvantage:
The consideration is confined to the items selected in advance and the topic is not dealt with as thoroughly as, for example, in the "problem-analysis scheme" (see pp. 124f.).

How?

The moderators put up a "two-part board" before the group. The headings of the individual parts (which can, for instance, be questions) depend on the topic to be dealt with and on the particular objectives of the group work. The important thing is that the participants be urged to keep their answers as concrete as possible.

The participants answer the question of each part by calling out; the moderators share the work of guiding the process and writing the replies down on the poster.

Tip: This scheme is ideal for work in small groups, when first thoughts on a topic (or on different topics) are to be developed simultaneously within a short time in order to further process them afterwards in the plenum.

When?

In Step 4: "Handling the topic"

Handling

120

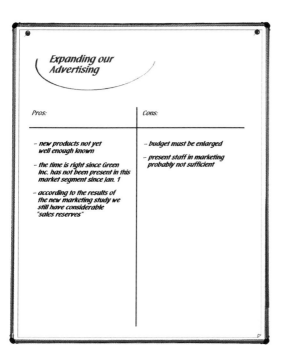

Expanding our Advertising

Pros:	Cons:
– new products not yet well enough known	– budget must be enlarged
– the time is right since Green Inc. has not been present in this market segment since Jan. 1	– present staff in marketing probably not sufficient
– according to the results of the new marketing study we still have considerable "sales reserves"	

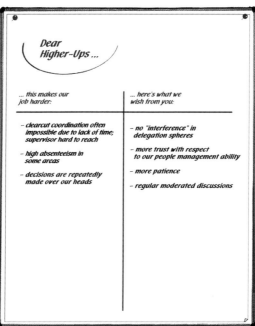

Dear Higher-Ups ...

... this makes our job harder:	... here's what we wish from you:
– clearcut coordination often impossible due to lack of time; supervisor hard to reach	– no "interference" in delegation spheres
– high absenteeism in some areas	– more trust with respect to our people management ability
– decisions are repeatedly made over our heads	– more patience
	– regular moderated discussions

Fig. 42. "Two-part board"

What?

"Four-Part Board/Quadrants"

Why?

This is a great method for handling a topic in small groups. It serves to shed more light upon subtopics, to expose possible conflicts, to develop first approaches to solutions, etc.

Advantage:
The quadrants allow for a clear structure and enable a rapid preliminary treatment of the subject matter.

Disadvantage:
The consideration of the subject matter is confined to the items selected in advance and the topic is not dealt with as thoroughly as for example in the "problem-analysis scheme" (see pp. 124f.).

How?

The moderators place a "four-part board" before the group. The headings of the individual fields and the questions pertaining to them depend on the topic to be dealt with and on the particular objectives of the work in the group. The important thing is that the participants be urged to keep their answers as concrete as possible.

The participants answer the question in each quadrant by calling out; the moderators share the work of guiding the process and writing the answers down on the poster.

By the way: This scheme is ideal for work in small groups when first thoughts on a topic (or on different topics) are to be developed simultaneously within a short time in order to further process them afterwards in the plenum.

When?

IIn Step 4: "Handling the topic"

Handling

Work in the office/in the Field

What should our teamwork be like?	How do we experience our teamwork?
– trusing – unified/standardized – transparent for employees and customers	– often no understanding for pressing jobs in the field – poor flow of information: "the office" doesnt know what "the field" is doing, and vice versa
What should be done?	**What are the first steps to take?**
– job rotation between office and field work compulsory for all employees – establish clear rules, in detail	– work out standards – hire a "stand-in" – switch "office-Miller" and "field-Baker" for six month

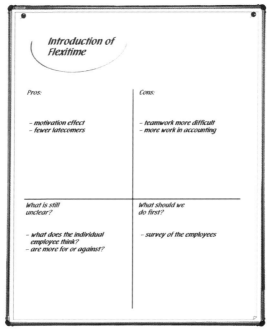

Introduction of Flexitime

Pros:	Cons:
– motivation effect – fewer latecomers	– teamwork more difficult – more work in accounting
What is still unclear?	**What should we do first?**
– what does the individual employee think? – are more for or against?	– survey of the employees

Fig. 43. "Quadrants"   **123**

What?

"Problem-Analysis Scheme" (PAS)

Why?

This method is especially suitable for intensive treatment of a topic. It serves to more clearly elucidate a selected (sub-)topic, to break a problem down into its several parts and to systematically describe it, to work out possible approaches to solving the problem, and to identify possible obstacles to solution.

Advantage:
The PAS sets forth a clear structure for the group work and provides a wealth of information.

Disadvantage:
This scheme is not all that easy to manage and is time-consuming.

How?

The moderators present to the group the problem-analysis scheme (PAS) in the form of a four-column table. The headings of the individual columns are given as questions. The participants answer the particular question when called upon; the moderators share the work of guiding the process and writing the answers down on the poster.

Hint for handling: To achieve a well-ordered arrangement, first of all enter one response in the first column and continue all the way across to the right. Then work from right to left. The second point is treated in the same way ….

When?

In Step 4: "Handling the topic"

Handling

124

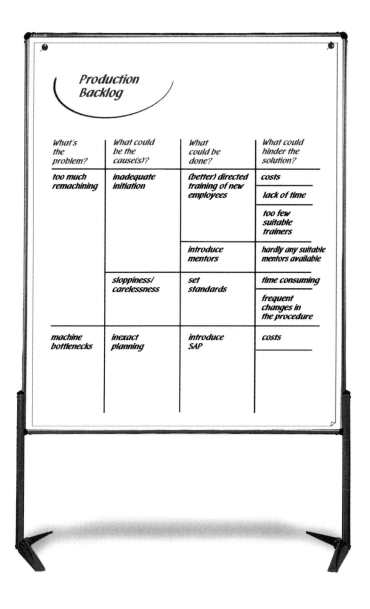

Production Backlog

What's the problem?	What could be the cause(s)?	What could be done?	What could hinder the solution?
too much remachining	inadequate initiation	(better) directed training of new employees	costs
			lack of time
			too few suitable trainers
		introduce mentors	hardly any suitable mentors available
	sloppiness/ carelessness	set standards	time consuming
			frequent changes in the procedure
machine bottlenecks	inexact planning	introduce SAP	costs

Fig. 44. Problem-analysis scheme

What?

"Cause–Effect Diagram"

Why?

A cause-effect diagram is good for the systematic analysis of the causes of a problem, especially when these can be quantitatively measured.

Advantage:
The pre-structuring of the problem landscape is a great help in the problem analysis. It focuses the group's attention on the given categories.

Disadvantage:
When searching for the solution to the problem every entry made in the diagram must be discussed again.

How?

The moderators set up before the group the rough structure of a flow-chart with a herring-bone pattern, the cause-effect diagram. The problem to be examined is entered at the "head" end. The four principal branches are labeled "Man," "Machine," "Method," and "Material." Then, as the information is called out, the moderators write down in the scheme what the group considers to be the causes of the problem.

One moderator guides the process while the other one visualizes the contributions for all to see.

When?

Step 4: "Handling the topic"

Handling

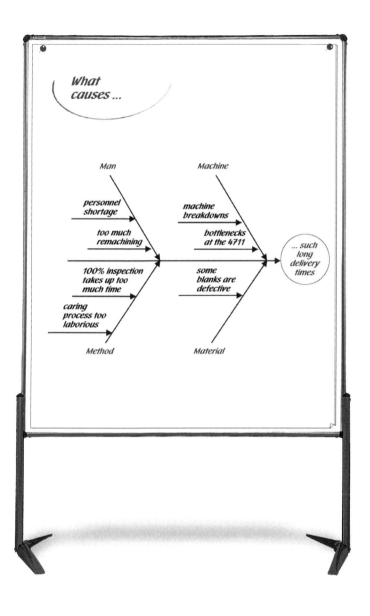

Fig. 45. Cause–effect diagram

What?

"Network Chart/Mind Map"

Why?

A network chart (similar to a "mind map") is especially well suited for delving further into a topic, for displaying organizational structures, and for clarifying relationships. It is a good method for "getting to the heart of the matter."

Advantages:
Wide range of application possibilities.

Disadvantages:
If there are a large number of items/entries, the representation can lose its clarity.

How?

The starting point of the network chart is always a circle placed in the center of the poster, with the keywords of the topic or problem visualized in the circle, either as a question or as part of a sentence. One example: "What are the duties of a moderator?"

The moderators ask the group to call out additions to the scheme, and they visualize the responses on the poster. The important thing here is for the principal items to be sought out and written down first of all, so that the picture grows from the inside to the outside.

When the initial question has been exhaustively dealt with, a new question is formulated for each of the items found. Supposing that we had arrived at an item "Leading the Group" in our example, then the next question could be: "What does leading the group entail?" This process continues until the topic has been handled sufficiently in keeping with the given objective.

When?

In Step 4: "Handling the topic"

Handling

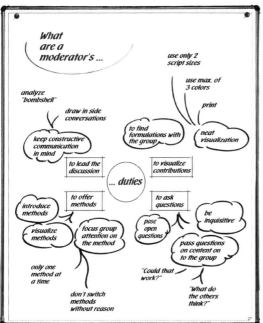

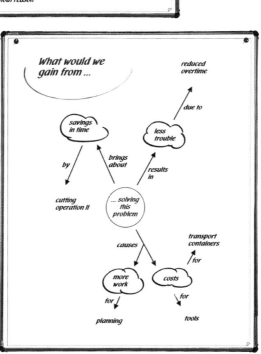

Fig. 46. Network chart

What?

"Matrix"

Why?

A matrix is suitable for handling a topic whenever the purpose is (and/or if it makes sense) to place data in relation to other data.

Advantages:
Tight structuring of the work. Relations and connections between single items of data are made clear.

Disadvantage:
The handling of the given task may be curtailed by the narrowed perspective dictated by the headings of the rows and columns.

How?

The moderators draft a matrix and label the rows and columns on the pin board. If possible and practical, they do this before working on it with the group, but otherwise together with the group.

The group then deals with the topic and fills in the individual fields. The moderators guide the discussion in the group and visualize the contributions made. Here, once more, a division of duties between the moderators suggests itself – one leading the discussion with the other in charge of the visualization.

When?

Primarily in Step 4: "Handling the topic;" but also for the "getting-to-know-you matrix" etc.

Handling

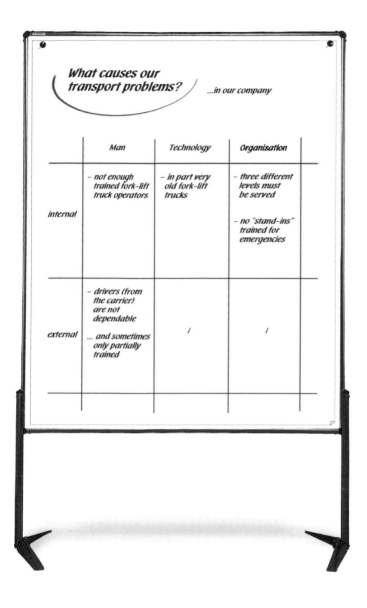

What causes our transport problems? ...in our company

	Man	Technology	Organization
internal	– not enough trained fork-lift truck operators	– in part very old fork-lift trucks	– three different levels must be served – no "stand-ins" trained for emergencies
external	– drivers (from the carrier) are not dependable ... and sometimes only partially trained	/	/

Fig. 47. Matrix

What?

"Flowchart"

Why?

A flowchart is an excellent way to handle a topic when a flow of events suggests itself for structuring the work, for example in a production or service process.

Advantage:
Clear structuring of the work

Disadvantage:
Possibly limits the perspective.

How?

The moderators work out the flow of events with the group or present a prepared one if it is common knowledge.

The group then works on the questions and problems pertaining to each individual step in the flow of events. The moderators share the work of guiding the process and simultaneously visualizing the participants' contributions on the poster.

For example, this method could be used to develop an optimized target flow of events for an actual flow of events previously found in an analysis.

When?

In Step 4: "Handling the topic"

Handling

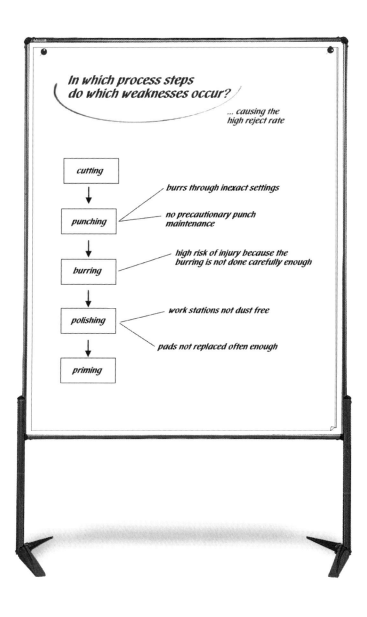

In which process steps do which weaknesses occur?

... causing the high reject rate

cutting

↓

punching — burrs through inexact settings

no precautionary punch maintenance

↓

burring — high risk of injury because the burring is not done carefully enough

↓

polishing — work stations not dust free

pads not replaced often enough

↓

priming

Fig. 48. Flowchart

What?

"Brainstorming"

Why?

Brainstorming is probably the best-known method of finding ideas.

Advantage:
You can find a lot of ideas within a short time.

Disadvantage:
For unpracticed groups it is difficult to refrain from immediately evaluating the thoughts and ideas.

How?

The moderators introduce the method on the basis of the visualized four basic principles, namely:

1. No criticism of your own thoughts or those of others!
2. Free and uninhibited expression of ideas, even unorthodox ones – "Go nuts"!
3. Take up and pursue the ideas of the others.
4. Come up with as many ideas as possible, without regard for their quality (quantity before quality).

After this you ask the group to process the problem visualized as a question on the pin board or flip chart, using the "called-out responses" method (see p. 110). At least ten minutes, but no more than twenty, should be spent collecting the ideas. Writing the contributions down for all to see is a valuable aid in making associations.

After the idea-collecting phase the result is evaluated, i.e., organized and examined for usefulness. It is advisable to take a break between these phases.

When?

In Step 4: "Handling the topic"

Handling

> **What could we do with our old tires?**
>
> – sell
>
> – recap
>
> – produce packing material
>
> – paint with bright colors
>
> – use for company kindergarten
>
> –design a play landscpae
>
> – give them to the town for playgrounds
>
> – build a tower

Fig. 49. Brainstorming

What?

"Chart of Measures to be Taken"

Why?

The purpose of the chart of measures to be taken is to guarantee that the group session is not devoid of results, but rather that it ends with concrete plans for which concrete measures to carry them out have also been agreed upon.

How?

The moderators set up a table before the group, with column headings that have already been visualized. The point is to determine ...

... who
... does what
... with which aim (why)
... by/from when and
... how checks on the implementation are to be made, and/
      or how the others are to receive progress reports.

At the end of the work together the group must concur on which of the envisaged measures/solutions they will concretely pursue further and what specific measures result from this.

The moderators' task is to ensure that the single measures are formulated as clearly as possible and that they can be put into effect by the group members themselves. This means that in each column only the names of those participating in the group can be entered and that concrete dates and deadlines must be set. The moderators do not assume any tasks relating to content!

When?

In Step 5: "Planning measures to be taken"

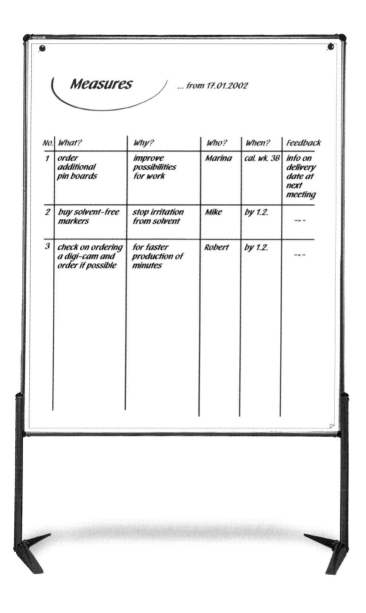

Measures ... from 17.01.2002

No.	What?	Why?	Who?	When?	Feedback
1	order additional pin boards	improve possibilities for work	Marina	cal. wk. 38	info on delivery date at next meeting
2	buy solvent-free markers	stop irritation from solvent	Mike	by 1.2.	-"-
3	check on ordering a digi-cam and order if possible	for faster production of minutes	Robert	by 1.2.	-"-

Fig. 50. Chart of measures to be taken

What?

"Mood Barometer"

Why?

As its name suggests, the mood barometer serves to make moods transparent and open to discussion.

How?

The moderators display a prepared poster or flip chart on which a scale that fits the particular situation offers each participant the opportunity to indicate his or her own personal mood at that moment.

The participants are then called upon to use an adhesive dot to visualize their momentary emotional state on the scale.

The overall mood is then discussed.

Note: This is a "single-dot" type of question.

When?

At any point in the moderation process, depending on the situation, but primarily in Step 6: "Conclusion"

If the mood barometer is repeated at fixed intervals (such as daily), it provides an overall view of the changes in mood in the group throughout the entire meeting.

Conclusion

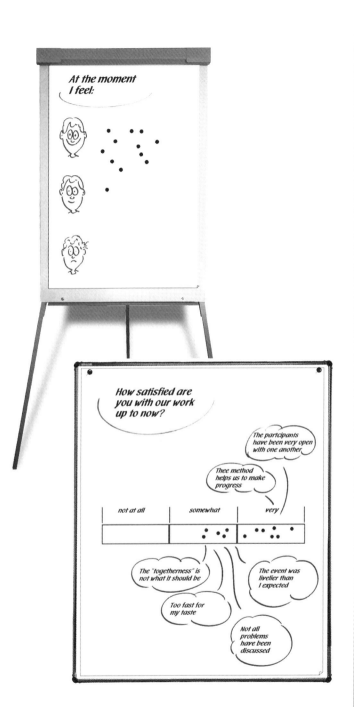

Fig. 51. Mood barometer

What?

"Flash"

Why?

This method serves to fix the momentary mood in the group as a "snapshot" and in this way to shed light on disruptive influences such as fatigue, excessive demands, or anger.

An additional possible use of this method is for the daily evaluation that reflects how the group views the outcome of the work and/or the atmosphere within the group.

How?

In keeping with its tradition, the "flash" is usually conducted without visualization.

Each participant gets an opportunity to say something about ...

    ... how she feels at the moment
    ... how satisfied he is with the result
    ... what she thought of the cooperation within the group

In this exercise the following rules should be observed:

a) each person has an opportunity to say something
b) each person says as much or as little as he or she wishes
c) the contributions are not commented on or discussed

The same rules apply for the moderators.

When?

In any step of the moderation, as the situation demands; but primarily in Step 6: "Conclusion"

3.4.4 Guiding a Moderation Process

The moderator is the specialist for methodology and process control. It is his job to steer the togetherness in the group, that is, to help it to become and remain capable of work.

He can do this for one thing by using "impeccable" working methods with regard to the "facts," and for another by competently guiding the emotional process of the group.

For orderly work on the subject matter he will take his bearings from the moderation cycle and the methods suggested for the substantive work. This "automatically" also results in a valuable contribution to the emotional guidance of the group.

The group emotional development does not orient itself per se toward the factual structure of the work, but rather it follows its own rhythm, which runs invisibly "beneath the surface." It is now up to the moderator to be a "synchronization aid" and to bring the emotional and factual phases into agreement with each other.

In addition to the "factual phases" (see pp. 92ff.), namely:

- Introduction
- Gathering
- Selecting
- Handling
- Planning
- Conclusion

there are also the emotional phases:

- **Orientation phase**
- **Work phase**
- **Closing phase**

1	2	3	4	5	6
Introduction	Gathering	Selecting	Handling	Planning	Conclusion
Orientation	**Work**				**Closing**

Fig. 52. Process phases

Phase 1: "Orientation"

In every (new) group each individual member will at first be uncertain about "what's going on here." Each person wants to know what "dangers" lie ahead for him and which persons or things he must pay (particular) attention to. This goes hand in hand with the fact that no one particularly enjoys being embarrassed, which is exactly what could happen if someone is not "in the picture." Thus the participant also wants to know how he should behave, if the others will accept him, what is expected of him, and what is frowned upon, in short: the rules that (will) apply in the group.

In this connection a "pecking order" is always established within a group. Things are settled such as who may say what to whom and how, whom one is willing to listen to, whose opinion is "less important" …

This is not openly settled, but is rather negotiated "behind the scenes" within the framework of the clarification of (apparently) important matters of content. But it must be done if the individual and hence the group is to be (fully) capable of working. The resulting structure generally does not remain unchanged, but at least it provides an initial support.

The moderator can (and should) actively influence this phase to help the group achieve its (full) working potential as quickly as possible. To do this he can:

- Make use of the time before the beginning!

  Who has never been in the situation of hardly having arrived before being hit by an "avalanche" of everything imaginable and unimaginable. Your fondest wish at this point (of physical presence) is simply to be permitted to (mentally) "arrive." This "arrival" includes letting go of what had been going on before and focusing on what is yet to come. The moderator can lend a helping hand on the emotional level. The proverbial conversation about the weather can be put to good use here. Its purpose is to establish contact, dispel uneasiness, and build up familiarity – to promote mutual trust and liking. Each person should be able to discover "whom he or she is dealing with."

● Settle everything that can be formally settled!

As already discussed in 'Step 1: "Introduction"', p. 92, this includes:

– Opening the session
– Clarifying expectations
– Voting on/formulating the objectives
– Voting on/setting forth the methodology
– Settling the matter of taking minutes

● Create a positive working environment!

Only if constructive rules for getting along with each other are successfully established (due to the moderator) will a positive and productive working climate be created. To achieve this goal the moderator can demonstrate that each participant is important, by trying …

… to connect with all participants by eye contact and questions

… to address the participants by name, to take their contributions seriously, to ask comprehension questions

… to actively listen, to concentrate on the participant speaking at the moment, to let him or her have his or her say and to endeavor to understand his or her contribution

Phase 2: "Work"

If necessary, the moderator will lengthen the orientation phase somewhat, to prevent it from running over into the "gathering topics" phase and to keep from still having to deal with matters of orientation and struggles for status during this work step. There is then a smooth transition from the orientation phase to the work phase. The members of the group know "which way the wind blows," and they have found their (social/psychological) place in the group. Energies are now free for working together on the subject matter.

In any event, during the "work phase," the moderator must also perform (group) psychological duties in addition to factual tasks, i.e., "working through" the moderation cycle. These duties lie in two areas:

- providing communication/interaction aids and
- mastering problem situations

Providing Communication/Interaction Aids

Anyone can communicate with others; there is no one who cannot. Nevertheless, it is not all that easy to communicate skillfully. This is especially true in a group, and especially an unfamiliar one. Part of the moderator's task is to give the members of the group a helping hand in this. For example, either at the beginning of the session or in the course of the moderation, "as needed" so to speak, the moderator can suggest rules of conduct for working together and implement them if the group agrees. In addition to purely organizational agreements such as "no smoking in the meeting room," "rules of the game" that fix the ways and means of communication in the group can also be worked out. Rules that have proved themselves in practice are, for example:

- Disruptions have priority!

  If the working climate is not in order there is no point in continuing substantive work. This means that disruptions such as objections, anger, disunity, fatigue, and indifference must be dealt with. It is the responsibility of every group member, but above all the moderator, to recognize and address this problem.

This is not (always) easy, since it takes up time and evokes a conflict. To address a disruption the moderator can make use of the "feedback technique" and/or a "mood barometer" for evaluating the process as described on pages 138f. At any rate, the moderator must have at his command the "rules for giving feedback" and the "rules for accepting feedback" as described on pages 76ff. It may even be necessary to discuss these rules with the group (in advance), to permit thorough treatment of a disruption. To deal with a disruption it is necessary to talk about the situation (of the discussion); this is what we call **"meta-communication."**

⦿ Use the first person "I" and not "one"!

The purpose of this rule is to obligate every participant to assume responsibility for his or her comments and not to hide behind the impersonal "one."

⦿ Speak for yourself – not for others!

This rule is aimed at getting each person to speak in his or her own name and to refrain (as far as possible) from making interpretations. This then precludes speaking of what other people could, should or must … have seen, felt, meant ….

Each one should speak of that which he or she has seen … and/or should ask the other members of the group how they understood, experienced … something. In this way the communication within the group becomes more authentic and clear; the interaction among the members becomes more open and honest.

Mastering Difficult Situations

Difficult situations (for the moderator as well) can arise in any group. Overcoming them in a positive and constructive way is crucial for the success of the moderation. Here are some examples:

- The group won't cooperate

  If the group does not cooperate, for instance if the participants are reluctant to supply any substantive contributions and/or instead they display destructive behavior, the moderator must leave the plane of substantive work and announce a "disruption" (see above, pp. 144f.). He will mention the situation, inquire about causes and search with the group for a possibility for meaningful (further) work.

- The group does not accept the proposed methodology

  If the group does not accept the procedure proposed by the moderator, the moderator must accept this for the time being. He will inquire after reasons for the rejection and attempt to understand them. If the group simply has a better idea for the procedure, the moderator will take it up. However, when something like this happens the reason behind it usually has more to do with anxieties about which the individual is not necessarily even aware and which therefore are not (or cannot be) verbalized. It then becomes the moderator's task to find a procedure – with and for the group – that the members of the group (can) accept.

  But: Do not needlessly cast doubt on your own methodology!

- The methodology doesn't work

Before commencing work the group agrees on how to proceed; the moderator proposes suitable methods. If, in the course of the work, it becomes clear that the group is not making progress with the working method selected, but rather that it is "going around in circles," "has got bogged down," ... then as a rule it is best for the moderator to take this up and search with the group for a different, more effective procedure instead of getting in even deeper, perhaps through fear of embarrassment. To be sure the saying "all's well that ends well" also applies here, and the moderator could hope that somehow he will manage to complete the work with the group by pressing on; nonetheless, it is generally better to make a methodical clean cut and (after a short break) to take a new approach.

- Time is running out

In spite of a schedule, time can run short. To keep this from putting everyone under pressure, the moderator must mention the lack of time early and clarify how the group wants to deal with it. By no means should there be any "open ends;" this means that clear agreements on how to proceed must be made for all topics that are to be (should be) handled (for more on this see "Chart of measures to be taken," pp. 136f.).

If it should become necessary to (temporarily) greatly streamline the process of handling the topics, the moderator can make use of the technique of "visual discussion."

Visual Discussion

The consistent, running visualization of all thoughts expressed in the group during a moderation, be it on cards or directly on paper, is called "visual discussion." It is the way of working in which a discussion is conducted by means of visualization. Each person virtually talks to the pin board and not (directly) to the others in the group. The group "weaves the web" (draws a network chart) of what is said with the aid of the visualization by the moderator.

In a "normal" moderation process the moderator will not (and cannot) put everything to paper as it arises in a lively dialogue. Contrary to this, in the visual discussion that is precisely the goal, to focus and direct the discussion to one particular concrete item. "Leaps" of thought are not possible.

Extreme visual discussion forces concentration on what is essential. However, it also "gags" the discourse and hence the emotional contact among the participants. It is therefore important not to overdo this type of process control.

The visualization method best suited for this is the "network chart" (similar to mind mapping, see pp. 128f.).

In the visual discussion the moderator will …

… first of all briefly introduce the methodology (as always); i.e., he will explain:

"I suggest that we try to put everything in a network chart. By that I mean …

… immediately examine each piece of volunteered information in terms of its relevance to the topic/aspect being discussed at the moment:

"Where should I add that?" – "How should I formulate it?

● Personal attacks are made

The best way for the moderator to face personal attacks in the form of unprofessional and/or emotionally laden, ironic, or even sarcastic remarks addressed to other members of the group or to the moderator is to make the contribution objective by being specific. This means that he does not react with a reprimand or a counterattack. He takes the contribution seriously and asks probing questions such as how the remark is to be understood, what is meant by it or where the speaker considers the relation to the topic to lie, what the group is supposed to do with it, … . As a rule, the "attacker" will himself become aware of his destructiveness and will "come to his senses;" in stubborn cases the moderator will …

… request a personal conversation in the next break and settle the matter with the person in question. If the conflict is between two participants he will

… ask for a personal conversation with both "squabblers" and clarify the situation. If this is not possible he will have to

… interrupt/terminate the substantive work and pursue meta-communication with the group (for more on this see pp. 145f.).

● A chatterbox dominates the group

One of the moderator's duties is to see that every participant is involved. This means, for example, that he repeatedly encourages "quiet ones" to participate by addressing them directly and asking (follow-up) questions. This is made more difficult if one member of the group elbows his way to the forefront with frequent and (over-)exhaustive contributions to the point that he can hardly be stopped. Since as a rule such behavior is a front hiding a strong desire for attention and recognition, the moderator can have a calming effect first of all by showing that he takes this person and his comments seriously by clearly acknowledging him, and secondly by methodically steering away from him. For this purpose he could, for example …

… interrupt the comments and try to abbreviate them by attempting to "get to the point" with specific questions;
… visualize the main point of the contribution as he goes along (see p. 148, "Visual Discussion");
… let the group give their opinions on what is said;
… not permit one or another contribution to be made to begin with, by pointedly addressing other participants, such as the "quiet ones."

Note: You will find a detailed account of this "delicate" area of moderating in: Seifert, Josef W., Moderation & Kommunikation, GABAL Verlag, Offenbach 1999.

Phase 3: "Closing"
Depending on the amount of time they have spent working together, the contents of the work, and the results achieved, the participants will shift into a more or less intensive parting mood towards the end of the moderation. This phase of the group is marked by …

… the desire not to leave any loose ends,
… doubts as to whether in practice everything will work out as envisioned here, and
… thoughts about what the individual has to do after this gathering.

The participants should leave the meeting in a positive mood and with the firm intention of putting the measures resolved into action. The moderator can/should/must now …

● take care that nothing (with regard to content) is left open.

The topics/aspects gathered in step 2 of the moderation cycle must have been dealt with by the end of the meeting! Of course, in reality it can happen that the time frame is not sufficient. However, it is a cardinal error of moderation to collect topics (or aspects) and then, due to a lack of time, to leave them open. But what should be done if time runs out?

In any event the group must come to an agreement on how they are to deal with untreated items that cannot be (thoroughly) dealt with due to a lack of time. However, this should not be done under pressure "at the last minute," but rather as soon as it becomes apparent that time is growing short. The decisions on this are then noted as a measure to be taken (see pp. 95f. and 136f.).

● reflect on the process with the group.

Reflection on the group process (see pp. 75ff. and p. 96) and/or the momentary situation gives each member of the group the opportunity to say something more to the moderator and/or to the group, and it helps the individual to "let go" and take leave (mentally and emotionally as well).

● thank the participants.

Thanking the participants is (as experience shows) neither a matter of course nor a meaningless utterance. Without the constructive cooperation of the members of the group the moderator would not have been able to fulfill his obligation to lead the group to its goal. He would not even have been able to put a clear objective down on paper. Moderation needs partnership. It requires both sides for success: one who leads and those who follow.

● dismiss the participants on a positive note.

The participants should leave the meeting (if at all possible) in a positive mood. The final scene/the closing remarks should be, according to the situation, as optimistic as possible. A sip of champagne or "merely" a positive final statement could be part of this.

By the way: It is (almost) always possible to close on a positive note!

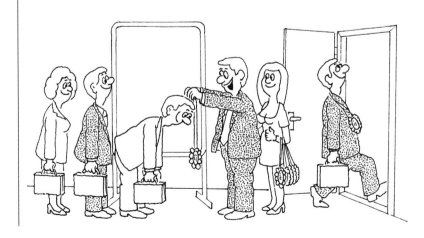

3.4.5 Excursion into Moderating a Discussion

Leading a discussion or meeting is basically nothing other than moderating a group session. There is a difference in practice, primarily because in a "classic" discussion …

- … moderation media, especially pin boards, are not/ cannot be used, and therefore
- … moderation methods can hardly be used for a discussion,
- … the moderator is usually not an uninvolved third party but the "problem-owner," the project leader or even his or her superior

To be able to conduct moderated discussions you must therefore first create the appropriate conditions with regard to "hardware" (see Section 3.4.2 "Moderation Aids").

Even if it should become necessary in a discussion – perhaps because of the large amount of written material required – to work sitting at tables and at least to this extent to deviate from the "customs" of the "classic" moderation, it is nevertheless possible to use moderation methods for the discussion.

There are no rigid rules on what methodology should be used for a specific phase of the discussion. However, we would like to encourage you to use moderation methods or some of them for your discussion routine. Here are a few …

Tips on Moderating a Discussion:

In your capacity as leader you should definitely have a preconceived notion of the methodology with which you would like to lead the group to its goal in the discussion. Don't be content with planning only the first steps – if at all possible, think the methodic course of the session all the way through to the end.

Introduce your method at the beginning of the discussion and adhere to it throughout the session.

No time to prepare for the discussion? At the very beginning of the session, agree with the participants on objectives and procedure.

If the items on the agenda have not already been fixed beforehand, they must be gathered at the beginning of the meeting (no discussion of methodology without concrete topics and objectives!). A suitable method for this would be the "called-out response" question (p. 110).

To set priorities, the order of the topics can then be determined with a "multi-dot question" (p. 118).

In problem-solving discussions, draft several alternative solutions before making a decision. Possible methods for this: brainstorming (p. 134) and the "two-part board" (p. 120).

A decision can be arrived at by mutual consent or with a "multi-dot question."

At the end of the discussion make certain that clear agreements have been reached; together with the participants, set up a "plan of measures to be taken" or a "plan of action."

... and what was that about a "disinterested third party"?

If you, in your capacity as moderator or leader of the discussion, are not in the happy situation of being able to act as uninvolved with the content of the discussion, you should try, as much as possible, to separate the two roles "party" and "moderator." You can do this:

A) **Nonverbally,** by standing whenever you are acting as the moderator and sitting whenever you contribute to the content of the discussion.

B) **Verbally,** by introducing your contributions to the content of the discussion with words such as *"For me as head of the XYZ department it would be important in this regard ..."* and your moderation steps with words such as *"Methodologically I can imagine that we first ..."* or *"What would help us methodologically now?"*

Moderating a Discussion *
as seen in a problem-solving discussion

Moderation methods can also be used for discussions. Here is an example:

Moderations Step	Discussion Phase	Moderation Methods for the Discussion (for example)
Introduction	Opening	Seating arrangement in semi-circle or U-shape. Visualization of topic, objectives and procedural steps on flip chart or pin board; Survey of expectations.
Gathering topics	Agreeing on agenda	Setting up a topic store by visualizing the items on the agenda on a flip chart or pin board as they are called out.
Selecting a topic	Setting priorities	Multi-dot question on the topic memory.
Handling the topic	Gathering Info	Problem-analysis scheme
	Developing alternative solutions	Problem-analysis scheme
	Deciding	Multi-dot question
Planning measures to be taken	Planning	Schedule of measures, including settling the matter of taking minutes
Conclusion	Closing	Flash

Fig. 53. Moderating a discussion

* You will find a detailed treatment of this subject matter in: Seifert, Josef W., Besprechungs-Modcration, GABAL Verlag, 6. Auflage, Offenbach 2000

3.5 After the Moderation

3.5.1 Personal Follow-Up

After the work with the group, the moderator (with the co-moderator, if any) will reflect on the course of the work and ask himself what now has to be done and how to proceed. This involves the three areas:

- Review
- Homework
- Further development

Review
To conclude the work with the group for yourself personally as moderator, and to "learn any lessons" from the events of the session, you will ask yourself questions such as:

- Have the objectives been fulfilled?
- Am I satisfied with the results?
- Am I satisfied with the course of events?
- Was my preparation good enough?

Homework
In the group meeting the moderator does not assume any tasks arising from the substantive work; however, he could volunteer to write up the minutes or to do other "homework" that arises from the organizational, methodical, or procedural level of the work. After the moderation he must concretely allow for this.

Further development
The work with the group usually does not end with the conclusion of the (first) moderation. The moderator must therefore consider what he must do for the further development and think about the appropriate steps to take. For example, he will make plans for the preparation of the next moderation.

3.5.2 Organizational Follow-Up

After the group meeting the work must also be followed up from an organizational point of view. At the very least, …

- … the room must be put in order
- … borrowed media, if any, must be returned
- … the minutes must be written up, and
- … the minutes must be distributed

The room should as far as possible look the same as when you first entered the room. Only then, in the case of a repetition, can you count on the owner of the room being kindly disposed to you.

If one of the media has become broken in any way, you should immediately(!) take action to remedy this; this is an extremely valuable part of the preparation for the next moderation.

Talking about the Minutes ...

Minutes can be divided fundamentally into:

Procedural minutes

Minutes of this type can be further divided into so-called "full minutes" and "part or short minutes."

For the full minutes, everything that is said during the meeting is written down word for word. They have the nature of "evidence." The classic example of full minutes are those of the sessions of legislative bodies.

Part or short minutes include only those items which is agreed upon should be included in the minutes. However, it always includes the results and decisions of the meeting.

Results minutes

These minutes include only the results/decisions of the gathering. The way in which the results were reached is not documented.

These minutes usually consist of typed pages. In contrast, for moderations a different type of minutes is usual, so-called "photo-minutes."

Photo-minutes

For photo-minutes, faithful copies of all the visualizations that are shown during the work process and/or that are newly created are used. The posters and flip-chart pages are simply photographed after the event and (copies of) the photos combined to form the minutes. Documentation (flip charts, transparencies, ...) of any short presentations that were made during the meeting accompanies the minutes as appendices. The contents of such minutes are equivalent to part or short minutes (procedural minutes). If just the plan of measures to be taken is used (see p. 136), the minutes have the character of results minutes. In both cases, however, the form is completely different. The digital form of typewritten characters is replaced by the analog form of pictures.

Photo-minutes have the following advantages compared to "normal" minutes:

✓ A separate person to take the minutes is not necessary; nothing must be written up neatly.

✓ The minutes are true documentation. The minutes are a faithful representation of the original flip charts and posters.

✓ The text does not need to be "approved" by the participants. They were all there as it was produced.

✓ The minutes are an emotional anchor for the participants. For this reason, photographs of scenes from the event can also be added.

However, there is no joy without sorrow: the catch is that the production of photo-minutes is technically not so easy.

The technical side of the production of photo-minutes

In order to produce professional photo-minutes, first of all everything on pin-board paper and flip-chart sheets that is to be included in the minutes is photographed using a high-resolution digital camera. This is easiest in a "photographic studio," i.e., a room in which the lighting conditions are constant (or can be made constant). In general, a fixed flash gun is useful.

After that the digital photographs are transferred to a PC and, if required, retouched using an image processing program such as "Adobe Photoshop." For extensive minutes it is desirable that the computer has sufficient RAM and hard disk capacity because digital photographs require a large amount of memory.

The original files can be printed out in either black and white or color and copied, or recorded on CD, or directly distributed by e-mail.

By the Way …

… only practice makes perfect!

The sultan himself was filled with delight: "As God is my witness; what a wonder, what a genius!" His vizier pointed out: "Your Highness, only practice makes perfect. The art of magic is the product of diligence and practice." The sultan frowned. His vizier's objection had spoiled his pleasure in the magic tricks. "You ungrateful worm! How can you claim that such skills come from practice? It is as I said: either one has the talent or one has none." He looked contemptuously at his vizier and cried: "At any rate you have none – off to the dungeon with you. There you can think about what I have said. A calf shall be your fellow prisoner so that you will have company of your own kind." From the very first day of his imprisonment the vizier practiced lifting the calf, and every day he carried it up and down the steps of the dungeon tower. The months passed by. The calf grew into a mighty bull and the vizier grew stronger with each day of practice. One day, the sultan remembered his prisoner. He had the vizier brought before him. At the sight of him the sultan's astonishment knew no bounds. "As God is my witness, what a wonder, what a genius!" The vizier, who bore the bull in his outstretched arms, answered with the same words as before: "Your Highness, only practice makes perfect. In your infinite mercy you gave me this beast for a companion. My strength is the product of my diligence and my practice."

I wish you much strength for coping with your visualization, presentation, and moderation tasks!

From: N. Peseschkian: Der Kaufmann und der Papagei (The Merchant and the Parrot), Fischer Taschenbuch, p. 117.

Literature

Argyle, Michael
Bodily Communication
Routledge
London 1990
ISBN 0415051142

Antons, Klaus
Praxis der Gruppendynamik
Verlag Hogrefe
Göttingen 2000
ISBN 3801713709

Cohn, Ruth
Von der Psychoanalyse zur themenzentrierten Interaktion
Klett-Cotta
Stuttgart 1997
ISBN 3608952888

Davidow, Ann
Let's Draw Animals
Grosset & Dunlap
New York, 1960
ISBN 0448029170

Fittkau, Bernd, et al.
Kommunizieren lernen (und umlernen)
Hahner Verlag
Aachen 1994
ISBN 3892941149

Glasl, Friedrich
Confronting Conflict
Hawthorn Press
Stroud UK 1999
ISBN 186989071X

Heller, Eva
Wie Farben auf Gefühl und Verstand wirken
Verlag Droemer Knaur
Munich 2000
ISBN 3426271745

Langenscheidt KG
OhneWörterBuch
Langenscheidt
Berlin and Munich 1999
ISBN 3468203942

Langer, Inghard, et al.
Sich verständlich ausdrücken
Ernst Reinhardt Verlag
Munich 1999
ISBN 3497014923

Klebert, Karin, et al.
Winning Group Results
Windmühle Verlag
Hamburg 2000
ISBN 3922789366

Schnelle-Cölln, Telse / Schnelle, Eberhard
Visualisieren in der Moderation
Windmühle Verlag
Hamburg 1998
ISBN 3922789501

Schrader, Einhard/Biehne, Joachim
Auswählen – Verdichten – Gestalten
Windmühle Verlag
Essen 1984

Seifert, Josef W./Kraus, Rolf
Mitarbeiter-Gruppen
GABAL Verlag
Offenbach 1996
ISBN 3923984944

Seifert, Josef W.
Besprechungs-Moderation
GABAL Verlag
Offenbach 2000; ISBN 393984936

Seifert, Josef W.
Moderation & Kommunikation
GABAL Verlag
Offenbach 1999; ISBN 389749003X

Svantesson, Ingemar
Mind Mapping & Memory
Kogan Page
London 1990
ISBN 0749401427

Watzlawick, Paul
Pragmatics Of Human Communication
W. W. Norton & Company
New York 1983
ISBN 0393010090

Will, Hermann (Ed.)
Mit den Augen lernen
Beltz Verlag
Weinheim and Basel 1994
ISBN 3407360142

Zelazny, Gene
Say it with Charts: The Executive's Guide to Visual Communication
McGraw-Hill
New York 2001
ISBN 007136997X

This bibliography lays no claim to completeness. Some of the books listed provided concrete ideas for this book. Others are intended as further reading. It would certainly be worthwhile "browsing" through one or the other. Have fun!

List of Figures

Index

*If you would like to
contact Josef W. Seifert
please send an e-mail to:*

j.w.seifert@businessmoderation.com

Notes

Notes

Notes